2023 Air Fryer

Cookbook for Beginners UK

1800 Days of Quick and Mouthwatering Air Fryer Recipes for Every Occasion, Elevate your cooking skills and create memorable dishes

Lola Sinclair

CONTENTS

INTRODUCTION

Hi, I'm Lola Sinclair, a home cook who loves to make good food. If you own an air fryer and don't know what you can do with it, this Air Fryer Cookbook will help you a lot. This cookbook offers 1600 mouth-watering recipes, each tailored to the Air Fryer's unique capabilities. From crispy snacks and savory main courses to decadent desserts, you'll discover a multitude of dishes that combine convenience, health, and flavor. We explore not just the frying capabilities, but also how to roast, grill, and bake with your Air Fryer. The Air Fryer Cookbook presents clear, step-by-step instructions for each recipe, along with expert tips to help you achieve perfect results every time. Whether you're looking for low-carb options, vegan delights, or indulgent comfort foods, this cookbook offers dishes to suit every preference and dietary requirement. Whether you are new to exploring air fryer techniques for the first time or a seasoned cook looking to expand your repertoire, The Air Fryer Cookbook is an invaluable resource. It's more than just a cookbook; it's a tool to inspire you to experiment, innovate and enjoy the journey of healthy cooking with your air fryer.

So open the pages, preheat your air fryer and embark on a culinary adventure that is sure to tantalise your taste buds while contributing to a healthier lifestyle!

Benefits of the Air Fryer

The Air Fryer is a versatile kitchen appliance that circulates hot air at high speed to cook and crisp food quickly and evenly. It gives you the ability to fry, grill and bake, making it an incredibly versatile addition to any kitchen. The air fryer offers the following benefits over ordinary home cooking

1. Reduced Oil Use: Air fryers use the circulation of hot air to cook food, which requires significantly less oil than traditional frying methods. This can result in healthier meals with less fat.

2. Quick and Efficient: Air fryers can cook food faster than conventional ovens because they heat food more evenly and require less preheating time.

3.Safer Than Deep Frying: Since they require less oil, air fryers can help reduce the risk of kitchen accidents related to deep frying, such as oil spills and splatters.

4.Flavorful Food: Despite using less oil, air fryers can still give food a tasty, crispy exterior while keeping the inside moist and tender.

5. Controlled Cooking: Air fryers often come with timers and temperature controls, which allow for precise cooking and prevent food from being undercooked or overcooked.

6. Reduced Acrylamide Formation: By using less oil, air fryers can help reduce the formation of acrylamide—a potentially harmful substance that can form in certain foods during high-heat cooking processes.

What you can cook in an Air Fryer?

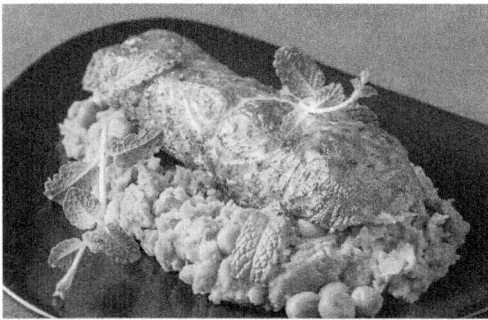

- **Fried Foods**

The Air Fryer's primary function is to mimic the results of deep frying. Foods like French fries, chicken wings, onion rings, and even donuts can be cooked with a fraction of the oil used in traditional frying.

- **Meat and Poultry**

You can cook various meats and poultry in an air fryer. Steaks, pork chops, and chicken breasts all come out beautifully seared on the outside and juicy on the inside. You can even roast a whole chicken.

- **Seafood**

Fish fillets, shrimp, and other types of seafood can be cooked in an air fryer quickly and to perfection.

- **Vegetables**

Roasted vegetables, including bell peppers, zucchini, broccoli, Brussels sprouts, and more, can be prepared in an air fryer. They turn out crispy and caramelized, with a delightful texture.

- **Baked Goods**

Surprisingly, air fryers can also work similarly to an oven. You can make small batches of cookies, muffins, and even personal pizzas.

- **Frozen Foods**

An Air Fryer can handle a variety of frozen foods, from mozzarella sticks and pizza rolls to fish sticks and fries. They cook up crisp and delicious without the need to thaw.

- **Reheating**

Air Fryers can also reheat leftovers more effectively than a microwave by restoring the food's original texture.

However, not all foods are suitable for air fryer. Delicate baked goods, foods with wet batters, or very small items like rice or corn kernels are typically not recommended for air frying.

Things to note when using an Air Fryer

Preheating:

While not necessary for all air fryers or recipes, preheating the air fryer for a few minutes before use can lead to better, more consistent results. It also helps in reducing cooking time.

Don't Overcrowd:

To ensure even cooking, avoid overcrowding the basket. If there's too much food, it may not cook evenly. Certain items may need to be cooked in batches.

Shake or Rotate:

For certain foods like fries or vegetables, shake the basket halfway through cooking to ensure even crispness. For larger items, consider flipping them for the same reason.

Check Food Frequently:

Air Fryers can cook food faster than traditional ovens, so check your food often to prevent burning, especially when trying a new recipe.

Cleaning:

Clean your air fryer regularly to avoid buildup of oil and food residue which can cause smoke during cooking. Most air fryers have parts that are dishwasher safe.

Safety:

Like any cooking appliance, air fryers can get very hot. Always use oven mitts or tongs to remove the basket, and be careful when reaching inside the unit.

How to clean an air fryer?

Cleaning your air fryer properly is essential to maintain its performance and longevity.

Always ensure that the air fryer is unplugged and cooled before you start cleaning to prevent accidental burns. Baskets, pans and any other removable parts are usually dishwasher safe. If you prefer to wash them by hand, use warm water, a mild dishwashing detergent and a non-abrasive sponge to clean these parts. Take care to avoid using metal utensils or abrasive cleaners that may scratch or damage the non-stick surfaces. Use a damp cloth or sponge to clean the interior of the air fryer. If there are stubborn residues, use a soft brush. Avoid using harsh or abrasive materials. Debris can sometimes collect on the heating element located inside the Air Fryer. Use a clean brush or cloth to carefully remove any food particles. Ensure that no damage is done to the heating coils. Depending on your use, give your air fryer a regular deep clean.

Hurry up and join the Air Fryer journey for a different kind of culinary experience!

Measurement Conversions

BASIC KITCHEN CONVERSIONS & EQUIVALENTS

DRY MEASUREMENTS CONVERSION CHART

3 TEASPOONS = 1 TABLESPOON = 1/16 CUP

6 TEASPOONS = 2 TABLESPOONS = 1/8 CUP

12 TEASPOONS = 4 TABLESPOONS = 1/4 CUP

24 TEASPOONS = 8 TABLESPOONS = 1/2 CUP

36 TEASPOONS = 12 TABLESPOONS = 3/4 CUP

48 TEASPOONS = 16 TABLESPOONS = 1 CUP

METRIC TO US COOKING CONVERSIONS

OVEN TEMPERATURES

120 °C = 250 °F

160 °C = 320 °F

180° C = 350 °F

205 °C = 400 °F

220 °C = 425 °F

LIQUID MEASUREMENTS CONVERSION CHART

8 FLUID OUNCES = 1 CUP = 1/2 PINT = 1/4 QUART

16 FLUID OUNCES = 2 CUPS = 1 PINT = 1/2 QUART

32 FLUID OUNCES = 4 CUPS = 2 PINTS = 1 QUART

 = 1/4 GALLON

128 FLUID OUNCES = 16 CUPS = 8 PINTS = 4 QUARTS = 1 GALLON

BAKING IN GRAMS

1 CUP FLOUR = 140 GRAMS

1 CUP SUGAR = 150 GRAMS

1 CUP POWDERED SUGAR = 160 GRAMS

1 CUP HEAVY CREAM = 235 GRAMS

VOLUME

1 MILLILITER = 1/5 TEASPOON

5 ML = 1 TEASPOON

15 ML = 1 TABLESPOON

240 ML = 1 CUP OR 8 FLUID OUNCES

1 LITER = 34 FL. OUNCES

WEIGHT

1 GRAM = .035 OUNCES

100 GRAMS = 3.5 OUNCES

500 GRAMS = 1.1 POUNDS

1 KILOGRAM = 35 OUNCES

US TO METRIC COOKING CONVERSIONS

1/5 TSP = 1 ML

1 TSP = 5 ML

1 TBSP = 15 ML

1 FL OUNCE = 30 ML

1 CUP = 237 ML

1 PINT (2 CUPS) = 473 ML

1 QUART (4 CUPS) = .95 LITER

1 GALLON (16 CUPS) = 3.8 LITERS

1 OZ = 28 GRAMS

1 POUND = 454 GRAMS

BUTTER

1 CUP BUTTER = 2 STICKS = 8 OUNCES = 230 GRAMS = 8 TABLESPOONS

WHAT DOES 1 CUP EQUAL

1 CUP = 8 FLUID OUNCES

1 CUP = 16 TABLESPOONS

1 CUP = 48 TEASPOONS

1 CUP = 1/2 PINT

1 CUP = 1/4 QUART

1 CUP = 1/16 GALLON

1 CUP = 240 ML

BAKING PAN CONVERSIONS

1 CUP ALL-PURPOSE FLOUR = 4.5 OZ

1 CUP ROLLED OATS = 3 OZ 1 LARGE EGG = 1.7 OZ

1 CUP BUTTER = 8 OZ 1 CUP MILK = 8 OZ

1 CUP HEAVY CREAM = 8.4 OZ

1 CUP GRANULATED SUGAR = 7.1 OZ

1 CUP PACKED BROWN SUGAR = 7.75 OZ

1 CUP VEGETABLE OIL = 7.7 OZ

1 CUP UNSIFTED POWDERED SUGAR = 4.4 OZ

BAKING PAN CONVERSIONS

9-INCH ROUND CAKE PAN = 12 CUPS

10-INCH TUBE PAN =16 CUPS

11-INCH BUNDT PAN = 12 CUPS

9-INCH SPRINGFORM PAN = 10 CUPS

9 X 5 INCH LOAF PAN = 8 CUPS

9-INCH SQUARE PAN = 8 CUPS

Breakfast & Snacks And Fries Recipes

<u>Whole Mini Peppers</u>

Servings: 2
Cooking Time:xx
Ingredients:

- 9 whole mini (bell) peppers
- 1 teaspoon olive oil
- ¼ teaspoon salt

Directions:

1. Preheat the air-fryer to 180°C/350°F.
2. Place the peppers in a baking dish that fits in for your air-fryer and drizzle over the oil, then sprinkle over the salt.
3. Add the dish to the preheated air-fryer and air-fry for 10–12 minutes, depending on how 'chargrilled' you like your peppers.

<u>Courgette Fries</u>

Servings: 2
Cooking Time:xx
Ingredients:

- 1 courgette/zucchini
- 3 tablespoons plain/all-purpose flour (gluten-free if you wish)
- ¼ teaspoon salt
- ¼ teaspoon freshly ground black pepper
- 60 g/¾ cup dried breadcrumbs (gluten-free if you wish; see page 9)
- 1 teaspoon dried oregano
- 20 g/¼ cup finely grated Parmesan
- 1 egg, beaten

Directions:

1. Preheat the air-fryer to 180°C/350°F.
2. Slice the courgette/zucchini into fries about 1.5 x 1.5 x 5 cm/⅝ x ⅝ x 2 in.
3. Season the flour with salt and pepper. Combine the breadcrumbs with the oregano and Parmesan.
4. Dip the courgettes/zucchini in the flour (shaking off any excess flour), then the egg, then the seasoned breadcrumbs.
5. Add the fries to the preheated air-fryer and air-fry for 15 minutes. They should be crispy on the outside but soft on the inside. Serve immediately.

<u>Mexican Breakfast Burritos</u>

Servings: 6
Cooking Time:xx
Ingredients:

- 6 scrambled eggs
- 6 medium tortillas
- Half a minced red pepper
- 8 sausages, cut into cubes and browned
- 4 pieces of bacon, pre-cooked and cut into pieces
- 65g grated cheese of your choice
- A small amount of olive oil for cooking

Directions:

1. Into a regular mixing bowl, combine the eggs, bell pepper, bacon pieces, the cheese, and the browned sausage, giving everything a good stir
2. Take your first tortilla and place half a cup of the mixture into the middle, folding up the top and bottom and rolling closed
3. Repeat until all your tortillas have been used
4. Arrange the burritos into the bottom of your fryer and spray with a little oil
5. Cook the burritos at 170°C for 5 minutes

Breakfast Eggs & Spinach

Servings: 4
Cooking Time:xx
Ingredients:
- 500g wilted, fresh spinach
- 200g sliced deli ham
- 1 tbsp olive oil
- 4 eggs
- 4 tsp milk
- Salt and pepper to taste
- 1 tbsp butter for cooking

Directions:
1. Preheat your air fryer to 180ºC
2. You will need 4 small ramekin dishes, coated with a little butter
3. Arrange the wilted spinach, ham, 1 teaspoon of milk and 1 egg into each ramekin and season with a little salt and pepper
4. Place in the fryer 15 to 20 minutes, until the egg is cooked to your liking
5. Allow to cool before serving

Crunchy Mexican Breakfast Wrap

Servings: 2
Cooking Time:xx
Ingredients:
- 2 large tortillas
- 2 corn tortillas
- 1 sliced jalapeño pepper
- 4 tbsp ranchero sauce
- 1 sliced avocado
- 25g cooked pinto beans

Directions:
1. Take each of your large tortillas and add the egg, jalapeño, sauce, the corn tortillas, the avocado and the pinto beans, in that order. If you want to add more sauce at this point, you can
2. Fold over your wrap to make sure that nothing escapes
3. Place each wrap into your fryer and cook at 190ºC for 6 minutes
4. Remove your wraps and place in the oven, cooking for a further 5 minutes at 180ºC, until crispy
5. Place each wrap into a frying pan and crisp a little more on a low heat, for a couple of minutes on each side

Plantain Fries

Servings: 2
Cooking Time:xx
Ingredients:
- 1 ripe plantain (yellow and brown outside skin)
- 1 teaspoon olive oil
- ¼ teaspoon salt

Directions:
1. Preheat the air-fryer to 180ºC/350ºF.
2. Peel the plantain and slice into fries about 6 x 1 cm/2½ x ½ in. Toss the fries in oil and salt, making sure every fry is coated.
3. Tip into the preheated air-fryer in a single layer (you may need to cook them in two batches, depending on the size of your air-fryer) and air-fry for 13–14 minutes until brown on the outside and soft on the inside. Serve immediately.

Easy Cheese & Bacon Toasties

Servings: 2
Cooking Time:xx
Ingredients:

- 4 slices of sandwich bread
- 2 slices of cheddar cheese
- 5 slices of pre-cooked bacon
- 1 tbsp melted butter
- 2 slices of mozzarella cheese

Directions:

1. Take the bread and spread the butter onto one side of each slice
2. Place one slice of bread into the fryer basket, buttered side facing downwards
3. Place the cheddar on top, followed by the bacon, mozzarella and the other slice of bread on top, buttered side upwards
4. Set your fryer to 170°C
5. Cook for 4 minutes and then turn over and cook for another 3 minutes
6. Serve whilst still hot

Your Favourite Breakfast Bacon

Servings: 2
Cooking Time:xx
Ingredients:

- 4-5 rashers of lean bacon, fat cut off
- Salt and pepper for seasoning

Directions:

1. Line your air fryer basket with parchment paper
2. Place the bacon in the basket
3. Set the fryer to 200°C
4. Cook for 10 minutes for crispy. If you want it very crispy, cook for another 2 minutes

Breakfast Sausage Burgers

Servings: 2
Cooking Time:xx
Ingredients:

- 8 links of your favourite sausage
- Salt and pepper to taste

Directions:

1. Remove the sausage from the skins and use a fork to create a smooth mixture
2. Season to your liking
3. Shape the sausage mixture into burgers or patties
4. Preheat your air fryer to 260°C
5. Arrange the burgers in the fryer, so they are not touching each other
6. Cook for 8 minutes
7. Serve still warm

Potato Fries

Servings: 2
Cooking Time:xx
Ingredients:

- 2 large potatoes (baking potato size)
- 1 teaspoon olive oil
- salt

Directions:

1. Peel the potatoes and slice into fries about 5 x 1.5cm/¾ x ¾ in. by the length of the potato. Submerge the fries in a bowl of cold water and place in the fridge for about 10 minutes.
2. Meanwhile, preheat the air-fryer to 160°C/325°F.
3. Drain the fries thoroughly, then toss in the oil and season. Tip into the preheated air-fryer in a single layer (you may need to cook them in two batches, depending on the size of your air-fryer). Air-fry for 15 minutes, tossing once during cooking by shaking the air-fryer drawer, then increase the temperature of the air-fryer to 200°C/400°F and cook for a further 3 minutes. Serve immediately.

Potato & Chorizo Frittata

Servings: 2
Cooking Time:xx
Ingredients:

- 3 eggs
- 1 sliced chorizo sausage
- 1 potato, boiled and cubed
- 50g feta cheese
- 50g frozen sweetcorn
- A pinch of salt
- 1 tbsp olive oil

Directions:

1. Add a little olive oil to the frying basket
2. Add the corn, potato, and sliced chorizo to the basket
3. Cook at 180°C until the sausage is a little brown
4. In a small bowl, beat together the eggs with a little seasoning
5. Pour the eggs into the pan
6. Crumble the feta on top
7. Cook for 5 minutes
8. Remove and serve in slices

Healthy Stuffed Peppers

Servings: 2
Cooking Time:xx
Ingredients:

- 1 large bell pepper, deseeded and cut into halves
- 1 tsp olive oil
- 4 large eggs
- Salt and pepper to taste

Directions:

1. Take your peppers and rub a little olive oil on the edges
2. Into each pepper, crack one egg and season with salt and pepper
3. You will need to insert a trivet into your air fryer to hold the peppers, and then arrange the peppers evenly
4. Set your fryer to 200°C and cook for 13 minutes
5. Once cooked, remove and serve with a little more seasoning, if required

Breakfast Doughnuts

Servings: 4
Cooking Time:xx
Ingredients:
- 1 packet of Pillsbury Grands
- 5 tbsp raspberry jam
- 1 tbsp melted butter
- 5 tbsp sugar

Directions:
1. Preheat your air fryer to 250ºC
2. Place the Pillsbury Grands into the air fryer and cook for around 5m minutes
3. Remove and place to one side
4. Take a large bowl and add the sugar
5. Coat the doughnuts in the melted butter, coating evenly
6. Dip into the sugar and coat evenly once more
7. Using an icing bag, add the jam into the bag and pipe an even amount into each doughnut
8. Eat warm or cold

Cumin Shoestring Carrots

Servings: 2
Cooking Time:xx
Ingredients:
- 300 g/10½ oz. carrots
- 1 teaspoon cornflour/cornstarch
- 1 teaspoon ground cumin
- ¼ teaspoon salt
- 1 tablespoon olive oil
- garlic mayonnaise, to serve

Directions:
1. Preheat the air-fryer to 200ºC/400ºF.
2. Peel the carrots and cut into thin fries, roughly 10 cm x 1 cm x 5 mm/4 x ½ x ¼ in. Toss the carrots in a bowl with all the other ingredients.
3. Add the carrots to the preheated air-fryer and air-fry for 9 minutes, shaking the drawer of the air-fryer a couple of times during cooking. Serve with garlic mayo on the side.

Patatas Bravas

Servings: 4
Cooking Time:xx
Ingredients:
- 300g potatoes
- 1 tsp garlic powder
- 1 tbsp avocado oil
- 1 tbsp smoked paprika
- Salt and pepper to taste

Directions:
1. Peel the potatoes and cut them into cubes
2. Bring a large saucepan of water to the boil and add the potatoes, cooking for 6 minutes
3. Strain the potatoes and place them on a piece of kitchen towel, allowing to dry
4. Take a large mixing bowl and add the garlic powder, salt, and pepper and add the avocado oil, mixing together well
5. Add the potatoes to the bowl and coat liberally
6. Place the potatoes into the basket and arrange them with space in-between
7. Set your fryer to 200ºC
8. Cook the potatoes for 15 minutes, giving them a shake at the halfway point
9. Remove and serve

Toad In The Hole, Breakfast Style

Servings: 4
Cooking Time:xx
Ingredients:

- 1 sheet of puff pastry (defrosted)
- 4 eggs
- 4 tbsp grated cheese (cheddar works well)
- 4 slices of cooked ham, cut into pieces
- Chopped fresh herbs of your choice

Directions:

1. Preheat your air fryer to 200ºC
2. Take your pastry sheet and place it on a flat surface, cutting it into four pieces
3. Take two of the pastry sheets and place them inside your fryer, cooking for up to 8 minutes, until done
4. Remove the pastry and flatten the centre down with a spoon, to form a deep hole
5. Add a tablespoon of the cheese and a tablespoon of the ham into the hole
6. Crack one egg into the hole
7. Return the pastry to the air fryer and cook for another 6 minutes, or until the egg is done as you like it
8. Remove and allow to cool
9. Repeat the process with the rest of the pastry remaining
10. Sprinkle fresh herbs on top and serve

Healthy Breakfast Bagels

Servings: 2
Cooking Time:xx
Ingredients:

- 170g self raising flour
- 120ml plain yogurt
- 1 egg

Directions:

1. Take a large mixing bowl, combine the flour and the yogurt to create a dough
2. Cover a flat surface with a little extra flour and set the dough down
3. Create four separate and even balls
4. Roll each ball out into a rope shape and form a bagel with each
5. Take a small mixing bowl and whisk the egg
6. Brush the egg over the top of the bagel
7. Arrange the bagels inside your fryer evenly
8. Cook at 170ºC for 10 minutes
9. Allow to cool before serving

Wholegrain Pitta Chips

Servings: 2
Cooking Time:xx
Ingredients:

- 2 round wholegrain pittas, chopped into quarters
- 1 teaspoon olive oil
- ½ teaspoon garlic salt

Directions:

1. Preheat the air-fryer to 180ºC/350ºF.
2. Spray or brush each pitta quarter with olive oil and sprinkle with garlic salt. Place in the preheated air-fryer and air-fry for 4 minutes, turning halfway through cooking. Serve immediately.

Cheese Scones

Servings:12
Cooking Time:xx
Ingredients:

- ½ teaspoon baking powder
- 210 g/1½ cups self-raising/self-rising flour (gluten-free if you wish), plus extra for dusting
- 50 g/3½ tablespoons cold butter, cubed
- 125 g/1½ cups grated mature Cheddar
- a pinch of cayenne pepper
- a pinch of salt
- 100 ml/7 tablespoons milk, plus extra for brushing the tops of the scones

Directions:

1. Mix the baking powder with the flour in a bowl, then add the butter and rub into the flour to form a crumblike texture. Add the cheese, cayenne pepper and salt and stir. Then add the milk, a little at a time, and bring together into a ball of dough.

2. Dust your work surface with flour. Roll the dough flat until about 1.5 cm/⅝ in. thick. Cut out the scones using a 6-cm/2½-in. diameter cookie cutter. Gather the offcuts into a ball, re-roll and cut more scones – you should get about 12 scones from the mixture. Place the scones on an air-fryer liner or a piece of pierced parchment paper.

3. Preheat the air-fryer to 180ºC/350ºF.

4. Add the scones to the preheated air-fryer and air-fry for 8 minutes, turning them over halfway to cook the other side. Remove and allow to cool a little, then serve warm.

Pitta Pizza

Servings: 2
Cooking Time:xx
Ingredients:

- 2 round wholemeal pitta breads
- 3 tablespoons passata/strained tomatoes
- 4 tablespoons grated mozzarella
- 1 teaspoon dried oregano
- 1 teaspoon olive oil
- basil leaves, to serve

Directions:

1. Preheat the air-fryer to 200ºC/400ºF.

2. Pop the pittas into the preheated air-fryer and air-fry for 1 minute.

3. Remove the pittas from the air-fryer and spread a layer of the passata/strained tomatoes on the pittas, then scatter over the mozzarella, oregano and oil. Return to the air-fryer and air-fry for a further 4 minutes. Scatter over the basil leaves and serve immediately.

Sauces & Snack And Appetiser Recipes

Bacon Smokies

Servings: 8
Cooking Time:xx
Ingredients:

- 150g little smokies (pieces)
- 150g bacon
- 50g brown sugar
- Toothpicks

Directions:

1. Cut the bacon strips into thirds
2. Put the brown sugar into a bowl
3. Coat the bacon with the sugar
4. Wrap the bacon around the little smokies and secure with a toothpick
5. Heat the air fryer to 170ºC
6. Place in the air fryer and cook for 10 minutes until crispy

Mini Aubergine Parmesan Pizza

Servings: 8
Cooking Time:xx
Ingredients:

- 1 aubergine, cut into ½ inch slices
- Salt to taste
- 1 egg
- 1 tbsp water
- 100g bread crumbs
- 75g grated parmesan
- 6 tbsp pizza sauce
- 50g sliced olives
- 75g grated mozzarella
- Basil to garnish

Directions:

1. Preheat air fryer to 160ºC
2. Mix egg and water together and in another bowl mix the breadcrumbs and parmesan
3. Dip the aubergine in the egg then coat with the breadcrumbs
4. Place in the air fryer and cook for 10 minutes
5. Spoon pizza sauce on the aubergine, add olives and sprinkle with mozzarella
6. Cook for about 4 minutes until cheese has melted

Stuffed Mushrooms

Servings: 24
Cooking Time:xx
Ingredients:

- 24 mushrooms
- ½ pepper, sliced
- ½ diced onion
- 1 small carrot, diced
- 200g grated cheese
- 2 slices bacon, diced
- 100g sour cream

Directions:

1. Place the mushroom stems, pepper, onion, carrot and bacon in a pan and cook for about 5 minutes
2. Stir in cheese and sour cream, cook until well combined
3. Heat the air fryer to 175ºC
4. Add stuffing to each of the mushrooms
5. Place in the air fryer and cook for 8 minutes

Tostones

Servings: 4
Cooking Time:xx
Ingredients:

- 2 unripe plantains
- Olive oil cooking spray
- 300ml of water
- Salt to taste

Directions:

1. Preheat the air fryer to 200ºC
2. Slice the tips off the plantain
3. Cut the plantain into 1 inch chunks
4. Place in the air fryer spray with oil and cook for 5 minutes
5. Remove the plantain from the air fryer and smash to ½ inch pieces
6. Soak in a bowl of salted water
7. Remove from the water and return to the air fryer season with salt cook for 5 minutes
8. Turn and cook for another 5 minutes

Salt And Vinegar Chips

Servings: 4
Cooking Time:xx
Ingredients:

- 6-10 Jerusalem artichokes, thinly sliced
- 150ml apple cider vinegar
- 2 tbsp olive oil
- Sea salt

Directions:

1. Soak the artichoke in apple cider vinegar for 20-30 minutes
2. Preheat the air fryer to 200ºC
3. Coat the artichoke in olive oil
4. Place in the air fryer and cook for 15 Minutes
5. Sprinkle with salt

Chicken & Bacon Parcels

Servings: 4
Cooking Time:xx
Ingredients:

- 2 chicken breasts, boneless and skinless
- 200ml BBQ sauce
- 7 slices of bacon, cut lengthwise into halves
- 2 tbsp brown sugar

Directions:

1. Preheat the air fryer to 220ºC
2. Cut the chicken into strips, you should have 7 in total
3. Wrap two strips of the bacon around each piece of chicken
4. Brush the BBQ sauce over the top and sprinkle with the brown sugar
5. Place the chicken into the basket and cook for 5 minutes
6. Turn the chicken over and cook for another 5 minutes

Onion Bahji

Servings: 8
Cooking Time:xx
Ingredients:

- 1 sliced red onion
- 1 sliced onion
- 1 tsp salt
- 1 minced jalapeño pepper
- 150g chickpea flour
- 4 tbsp water
- 1 clove garlic, minced
- 1 tsp coriander
- 1 tsp chilli powder
- 1 tsp turmeric
- ½ tsp cumin

Directions:

1. Place all ingredients in a bowl and mix well, leave to rest for 10 minutes
2. Preheat air fryer to 175ºC
3. Spray air fryer with cooking spray.
4. Form mix into bahji shapes and add to air fryer
5. Cook for 6 minutes turn and cook for a further 6 minutes

Italian Rice Balls

Servings: 2
Cooking Time:xx
Ingredients:

- 400g cooked rice
- 25g breadcrumbs, plus an extra 200g for breading
- 2 tbsp flour, plus an extra 2 tbsp for breading
- 1 tbsp cornstarch, plus an extra 3 tbsp for breading
- 1 chopped bell pepper
- 1 chopped onion
- 2 tbsp olive oil
- 1 tsp red chilli flakes
- 5 chopped mozzarella cheese sticks
- A little water for the breading
- Salt and pepper for seasoning

Directions:

1. Place the cooked rice into a bowl and mash with a fork. Place to one side
2. Take a saucepan and add the oil, salting the onion and peppers until they're both soft
3. Add the chilli flakes and a little salt and combine
4. Add the mixture to the mashed rice and combine
5. Add the 2 tbsp flour and 1 tbsp cornstarch, along with the 25g breadcrumbs and combine well
6. Use your hands to create balls with the mixture
7. Stuff a piece of the mozzarella inside the balls and form around it
8. Take a bowl and add the rest of the flour, corn starch and a little seasoning, with a small amount of water to create a thick batter
9. Take another bowl and add the rest of the breadcrumbs
10. Dip each rice ball into the batter and then the breadcrumbs
11. Preheat the air fryer to 220ºC
12. Cook for 6 minutes, before shaking and cooking for another 6 minutes

Tortellini Bites

Servings: 6
Cooking Time:xx
Ingredients:

- 200g cheese tortellini
- 150g flour
- 100g panko bread crumbs
- 50g grated parmesan
- 1 tsp dried oregano
- 2 eggs
- ½ tsp garlic powder
- ½ tsp chilli flakes
- Salt
- Pepper

Directions:

1. Cook the tortellini according to the packet instructions
2. Mix the panko, parmesan, oregano, garlic powder, chilli flakes salt and pepper in a bowl
3. Beat the eggs in another bowl and place the flour in a third bowl
4. Coat the tortellini in flour, then egg and then in the panko mix
5. Place in the air fryer and cook at 185ºC for 10 minutes until crispy
6. Serve with marinara sauce for dipping

Onion Pakoda

Servings: 2
Cooking Time:xx
Ingredients:
- 200g gram flour
- 2 onions, thinly sliced
- 1 tbsp crushed coriander seeds
- 1 tsp chilli powder
- ¾ tsp salt
- ¼ tsp turmeric
- ¼ tsp baking soda

Directions:
1. Mix all the ingredients together in a large bowl
2. Make bite sized pakodas
3. Heat the air fryer to 200°C
4. Line the air fryer with foil
5. Place the pakoda in the air fryer and cook for 5 minutes
6. Turn over and cook for a further 5 minutes

Garlic Cheese Bread

Servings: 2
Cooking Time:xx
Ingredients:
- 250g grated mozzarella
- 50g grated parmesan
- 1 egg
- ½ tsp garlic powder

Directions:
1. Line air fryer with parchment paper
2. Mix ingredients in a bowl
3. Press into a circle onto the parchment paper in the air fryer
4. Heat the air fryer to 175°C
5. Cook for 10 minutes

Pasta Chips

Servings: 2
Cooking Time:xx
Ingredients:
- 300g dry pasta bows
- 1 tbsp olive oil
- 1 tbsp nutritional yeast
- 1½ tsp Italian seasoning
- ½ tsp salt

Directions:
1. Cook the pasta for half the time stated on the packet
2. Drain and mix with the oil, yeast, seasoning and salt
3. Place in the air fryer and cook at 200°C for 5 minutes shake and cook for a further 3 minutes until crunchy

Mini Calzones

Servings: 16
Cooking Time:xx

Ingredients:

- Flour for rolling out the dough
- 1 round pizza dough
- 100g pizza sauce

Directions:

1. Roll out the dough to ¼ inch thick
2. Cut out 8-10 dough rounds using a cutter
3. Re-roll the dough and cut out another 6 rounds
4. Top each round with pizza sauce, cheese and pepperoni
5. Fold dough over and pinch the edges to seal
6. Heat the air fryer to 190ºC
7. Place the calzone in the air fryer and cook for about 8 minutes until golden brown

Air-fried Pickles

Servings: 4
Cooking Time:xx

Ingredients:

- 1/2 cup mayonnaise
- 2 tsp sriracha sauce
- 1 jar dill pickle slices
- 1 egg
- 2 tbsp milk
- 50g flour
- 50g cornmeal
- ½ tsp seasoned salt
- ¼ tsp paprika
- ¼ tsp garlic powder
- ⅛ tsp pepper
- Cooking spray

Directions:

1. Mix the mayo and sriracha together in a bowl and set aside
2. Heat the air fryer to 200ºC
3. Drain the pickles and pat dry
4. Mix egg and milk together, in another bowl mix all the remaining ingredients
5. Dip the pickles in the egg mix then in the flour mix
6. Spray the air fryer with cooking spray
7. Cook for about 4 minutes until crispy

Peppers With Aioli Dip

Servings: 4
Cooking Time:xx
Ingredients:

- 250g shishito peppers
- 2 tsp avocado oil
- 5 tbsp mayonnaise
- 2 tbsp lemon juice
- 1 minced clove of garlic
- 1 tbsp chopped parsley
- Salt and pepper for seasoning

Directions:

1. Take a medium bowl and combine the mayonnaise with the lemon juice, garlic, parsley and seasoning and create a smooth dip
2. Preheat the air fryer to 220ºC
3. Toss the peppers in the oil and add to the air fryer
4. Cook for 4 minutes, until the peppers are soft and blistered on the outside
5. Remove and serve with the dip

Roasted Almonds

Servings: 2
Cooking Time:xx
Ingredients:

- 1 tbsp soy sauce
- 1 tbsp garlic powder
- 1 tsp paprika
- ¼ tsp pepper
- 400g raw almonds

Directions:

1. Place all of the ingredients apart from the almonds in a bowl and mix
2. Add the almonds and coat well
3. Place the almonds in the air fryer and cook at 160ºC for 6 minutes shaking every 2 minutes

Pretzel Bites

Servings: 2
Cooking Time:xx
Ingredients:

- 650g flour
- 2.5 tsp active dry yeast
- 260ml hot water
- 1 tsp salt
- 4 tbsp melted butter
- 2 tbsp sugar

Directions:

1. Take a large bowl and add the flour, sugar and salt
2. Take another bowl and combine the hot water and yeast, stirring until the yeast has dissolved
3. Then, add the yeast mixture to the flour mixture and use your hands to combine
4. Knead for 2 minutes
5. Cover the bowl with a kitchen towel for around half an hour
6. Divide the dough into 6 pieces
7. Preheat the air fryer to 260ºC
8. Take each section of dough and tear off a piece, rolling it in your hands to create a rope shape, that is around 1" in thickness
9. Cut into 2" strips
10. Place the small dough balls into the air fryer and leave a little space in-between
11. Cook for 6 minutes
12. Once cooked, remove and brush with melted butter and sprinkle salt on top

Corn Nuts

Servings: 8
Cooking Time:xx
Ingredients:

- 1 giant white corn
- 3 tbsp vegetable oil
- 2 tsp salt

Directions:

1. Place the corn in a large bowl, cover with water and sit for 8 hours
2. Drain, pat dry and air dry for 20 minutes
3. Preheat the air fryer to 200ºC
4. Place in a bowl and coat with oil and salt
5. Cook in the air fryer for 10 minutes shake then cook for a further 10 minutes

Lumpia

Servings: 16
Cooking Time:xx
Ingredients:

- 400g Italian sausage
- 1 sliced onion
- 1 chopped carrot
- 50g chopped water chestnuts
- Cooking spray
- 2 cloves minced, garlic
- 2 tbsp soy sauce
- ½ tsp salt
- ¼ tsp ground ginger
- 16 spring roll wrappers

Directions:

1. Cook sausage in a pan for about 5 minutes. Add green onions, onions, water chestnuts and carrot cook for 7 minutes
2. Add garlic and cook for a further 2 minutes
3. Add the soy sauce, salt and ginger, stir to mix well
4. Add filling to each spring roll wrapper.
5. Roll over the bottom and tuck in the sides, continue to roll up the spring roll
6. Spray with cooking spray and place in the air fryer
7. Cook at 200ºC for 4 minutes turn and cook for a further 4 minutes

Spicy Chickpeas

Servings: 4
Cooking Time:xx
Ingredients:

- 1 can chickpeas
- 1 tbsp yeast
- 1 tbsp olive oil
- 1 tsp paprika
- 1 tsp garlic powder
- ½ tsp salt
- Pinch cumin

Directions:

1. Preheat air fryer to 180ºC
2. Combine all ingredients
3. Add to the air fryer and cook for 22 minutes tossing every 4 minutes until cooked

Poultry Recipes

Pizza Chicken Nuggets

Servings: 2
Cooking Time:xx
Ingredients:

- 60 g/¾ cup dried breadcrumbs (see page 9)
- 20 g/¼ cup grated Parmesan
- ½ teaspoon dried oregano
- ¼ teaspoon freshly ground black pepper
- 150 g/⅔ cup Mediterranean sauce (see page 102) or 150 g/5½ oz. jarred tomato pasta sauce (keep any leftover sauce for serving)
- 400 g/14 oz. chicken fillets

Directions:

1. Preheat the air-fryer to 180°C/350°F.
2. Combine the breadcrumbs, Parmesan, oregano and pepper in a bowl. Have the Mediterranean or pasta sauce in a separate bowl.
3. Dip each chicken fillet in the tomato sauce first, then roll in the breadcrumb mix until coated fully.
4. Add the breaded fillets to the preheated air-fryer and air-fry for 10 minutes. Check the internal temperature of the chicken has reached at least 74°C/165°F using a meat thermometer – if not, cook for another few minutes.
5. Serve with some additional sauce that has been warmed through.

Nashville Chicken

Servings: 4
Cooking Time:xx
Ingredients:

- 400g boneless chicken breast tenders
- 2 tsp salt
- 2 tsp coarsely ground black pepper
- 2 tbsp hot sauce
- 2 tbsp pickle juice
- 500g all purpose flour
- 3 large eggs
- 300ml buttermilk
- 2 tbsp olive oil
- 6 tbsp cayenne pepper
- 3 tbsp dark brown sugar
- 1 tsp chilli powder
- 1 tsp garlic powder
- 1 tsp paprika
- Salt and pepper to taste

Directions:

1. Take a large mixing bowl and add the chicken, hot sauce, pickle juice, salt and pepper and combine
2. Place in the refrigerator for 3 hours
3. Transfer the flour to a bowl
4. Take another bowl and add the eggs, buttermilk and 1 tbsp of the hot sauce, combining well
5. Press each piece of chicken into the flour and coat well
6. Place the chicken into the buttermilk mixture and then back into the flour
7. Allow to sit or 10 minutes
8. Preheat the air fryer to 193C
9. Whisk together the spices, brown sugar and olive oil to make the sauce and pour over the chicken tenders
10. Serve whilst still warm

Air Fryer Chicken Thigh Schnitzel

Servings: 4
Cooking Time:xx
Ingredients:
- 300g boneless chicken thighs
- 160g seasoned breadcrumbs
- 1 tsp salt
- ½ tsp ground black pepper
- 30g flour
- 1 egg
- Cooking spray

Directions:
1. Lay the chicken on a sheet of parchment paper and add another on top
2. Use a mallet or a rolling pin to flatten it down
3. Take a bowl and add the breadcrumbs with the salt and pepper
4. Place the flour into another bowl
5. Dip the chicken into the flour, then the egg, and then the breadcrumbs
6. Preheat air fryer to 190°C
7. Place the chicken into the air fryer and spray with cooking oil
8. Cook for 6 minutes

Healthy Bang Bang Chicken

Servings: 4
Cooking Time:xx
Ingredients:
- 500g chicken breasts, cut into pieces of around 1" in size
- 1 beaten egg
- 50ml milk
- 1 tbsp hot pepper sauce
- 80g flour
- 70g tapioca starch
- 1 ½ tsp seasoned starch
- 1 tsp garlic granules
- ½ tsp cumin
- 6 tbsp plain Greek yogurt
- 3 tbsp sweet chilli sauce
- 1 tsp hot sauce

Directions:
1. Preheat the air fryer to 190°C
2. Take a mixing bowl and combine the egg, milk and hot sauce
3. Take another bowl and combine the flour, tapioca starch, salt, garlic and cumin
4. Dip the chicken pieces into the sauce bowl and then into the flour bowl
5. Place the chicken into the air fryer
6. Whilst cooking, mix together the Greek yogurt, sweet chilli sauce and hot sauce and serve with the chicken

Chicken Kiev

Servings: 4
Cooking Time:xx
Ingredients:

- 4 boneless chicken breasts
- 4 tablespoons plain/all-purpose flour (gluten-free if you wish)
- 1 egg, beaten
- 130 g/2 cups dried breadcrumbs (gluten-free if you wish, see page 9)
- GARLIC BUTTER
- 60 g/4 tablespoons salted butter, softened
- 1 large garlic clove, finely chopped

Directions:

1. Mash together the butter and garlic. Form into a sausage shape, then slice into 4 equal discs. Place in the freezer until frozen.
2. Make a deep horizontal slit across each chicken breast, taking care not to cut through to the other side. Stuff the cavity with a disc of frozen garlic butter. Place the flour in a shallow bowl, the egg in another and the breadcrumbs in a third. Coat each chicken breast first in flour, then egg, then breadcrumbs.
3. Preheat the air-fryer to 180°C/350°F.
4. Add the chicken Kievs to the preheated air-fryer and air-fry for 12 minutes until cooked through. This is hard to gauge as the butter inside the breast is not an indicator of doneness, so test the meat in the centre with a meat thermometer – it should be at least 75°C/167°F; if not, cook for another few minutes.

Chicken Parmesan With Marinara Sauce

Servings: 4
Cooking Time:xx
Ingredients:

- 400g chicken breasts, sliced in half
- 250g panko breadcrumbs
- 140g grated parmesan cheese
- 140g grated mozzarella cheese
- 3 egg whites
- 200g marinara sauce
- 2 tsp Italian seasoning
- Salt and pepper to taste
- Cooking spray

Directions:

1. Preheat the air fryer to 200°C
2. Lay the chicken slices on the work surface and pound with a mallet or a rolling pin to flatten
3. Take a mixing bowl and add the panko breadcrumbs, cheese and the seasoning, combining well
4. Add the egg whites into a separate bowl
5. Dip the chicken into the egg whites and then the breadcrumbs
6. Cook for 7 minutes in the air fryer

Chicken Balls, Greek-style

Servings: 4
Cooking Time:xx
Ingredients:

- 500g ground chicken
- 1 egg
- 1 tbsp dried oregano
- 1.5 tbsp garlic paste
- 1 tsp lemon zest
- 1 tsp dried onion powder
- Salt and pepper to taste

Directions:

1. Take a bowl and combine all ingredients well
2. Use your hands to create meatballs - you should be able to make 12 balls
3. Preheat your air fryer to 260ºC
4. Add the meatballs to the fryer and cook for 9 minutes

Chicken & Potatoes

Servings: 4
Cooking Time:xx
Ingredients:

- 2 tbsp olive oil
- 2 potatoes, cut into 2" pieces
- 2 chicken breasts, cut into pieces of around 1" size
- 4 crushed garlic cloves
- 2 tsp smoked paprika
- 1 tsp thyme
- 1/2 tsp red chilli flakes
- Salt and pepper to taste

Directions:

1. Preheat your air fryer to 260ºC
2. Take a large bowl and combine the potatoes with half of the garlic, half the paprika, half the chilli flakes, salt, pepper and half the oil
3. Place into the air fryer and cook for 5 minutes, before turning over and cooking for another 5 minutes
4. Take a bowl and add the chicken with the rest of the seasonings and oil, until totally coated
5. Add the chicken to the potatoes mixture, moving the potatoes to the side
6. Cook for 10 minutes, turning the chicken halfway through

Thai Turkey Burgers

Servings: 4
Cooking Time:xx
Ingredients:

- 1 courgette/zucchini, about 200 g/7 oz.
- 400 g/14 oz. minced/ground turkey breast
- 35 g/½ cup fresh breadcrumbs (gluten-free if you wish)
- 1 teaspoon Thai 7 spice seasoning
- 1 teaspoon salt
- 1 teaspoon olive oil

Directions:

1. Coarsely grate the courgette/zucchini, then place in a piece of muslin/cheesecloth and squeeze out the water. Combine the grated courgette with all other ingredients except the olive oil, mixing together well. Divide the mixture into 4 equal portions and mould into burgers. Brush with oil.
2. Preheat the air-fryer to 190ºC/375ºC.
3. Add the turkey burgers to the preheated air-fryer and air-fry for 15 minutes, turning once halfway through cooking. Check the internal temperature of the burgers has reached at least 74ºC/165ºF using a meat thermometer – if not, cook for another few minutes and then serve.

Bbq Chicken Tenders

Servings: 6
Cooking Time:xx
Ingredients:
- 300g barbecue flavoured pork rinds
- 200g all purpose flour
- 1 tbsp barbecue seasoning
- 1 egg
- 400g chicken breast tenderloins
- Cooking spray

Directions:
1. Preheat the air fryer to 190ºC
2. Place the pork rinds into a food processor and blitz to a breadcrumb consistency, before transferring to a bowl
3. In a separate bowl, combine the flour and barbecue seasoning
4. Beat the egg in a small bowl
5. Take the chicken and first dip into the egg, then the flour, and then the breadcrumbs
6. Place the chicken into the air fryer and spray with cooking spray and cook for about 15 minutes

Grain-free Chicken Katsu

Servings: 4
Cooking Time:xx
Ingredients:
- 125 g/1¼ cups ground almonds
- ½ teaspoon salt
- ½ teaspoon garlic powder
- ½ teaspoon dried parsley
- ½ teaspoon freshly ground black pepper
- ¼ teaspoon onion powder
- ¼ teaspoon dried oregano
- 450 g/1 lb. mini chicken fillets
- 1 egg, beaten
- oil, for spraying/drizzling
- coriander/cilantro leaves, to serve
- KATSU SAUCE
- 1 teaspoon olive oil or avocado oil
- 1 courgette/zucchini (approx. 150 g/5 oz.), finely chopped
- 1 carrot (approx. 100 g/3½ oz.), finely chopped
- 1 onion (approx. 120 g/4½ oz.), finely chopped
- 1 eating apple (approx. 150 g/5 oz.), cored and finely chopped
- 1 teaspoon ground ginger
- 1 teaspoon ground turmeric
- 2 teaspoons ground cumin
- 2 teaspoons ground coriander
- 1½ teaspoons mild chilli/chili powder
- 1 teaspoon garlic powder
- 1½ tablespoons runny honey
- 1 tablespoon soy sauce (gluten-free if you wish)
- 700 ml/3 cups vegetable stock (700 ml/3 cups water with 1½ stock cubes)

Directions:
1. First make the sauce. The easiest way to ensure all the vegetables and apple are finely chopped is to combine them in a food processor. Heat the oil in a large saucepan and sauté the finely chopped vegetables and apple for 5 minutes. Add all the seasonings, honey, soy sauce and stock and stir well, then bring to a simmer and simmer for 30 minutes.
2. Meanwhile, mix together the ground almonds, seasonings and spices. Dip each chicken fillet into the beaten egg, then into the almond-spice mix, making sure each fillet is fully coated. Spray the coated chicken fillets with olive oil (or simply drizzle over).
3. Preheat the air-fryer to 180ºC/350ºF.
4. Place the chicken fillets in the preheated air-fryer and air-fry for 10 minutes, turning halfway through cooking. Check the internal temperature of the chicken has reached at least 74ºC/165ºF using a meat thermometer – if not, cook for another few minutes.
5. Blend the cooked sauce in a food processor until smooth. Serve the chicken with the Katsu Sauce drizzled over (if necessary, reheat the sauce gently before serving) and scattered with coriander leaves. Any unused sauce can be frozen.

Sticky Chicken Tikka Drumsticks

Servings: 4
Cooking Time:xx
Ingredients:
- 12 chicken drumsticks
- MARINADE
- 100 g/½ cup Greek yogurt
- 2 tablespoons tikka paste
- 2 teaspoons ginger preserve
- freshly squeezed juice of ½ a lemon
- ¾ teaspoon salt

Directions:
1. Make slices across each of the drumsticks with a sharp knife. Mix the marinade ingredients together in a bowl, then add the drumsticks. Massage the marinade into the drumsticks, then leave to marinate in the fridge overnight or for at least 6 hours.
2. Preheat the air-fryer to 200ºC/400ºF.
3. Lay the drumsticks on an air-fryer liner or a piece of pierced parchment paper. Place the paper and drumsticks in the preheated air-fryer. Air-fry for 6 minutes, then turn over and cook for a further 6 minutes. Check the internal temperature of the drumsticks has reached at least 75ºC/167ºF using a meat thermometer – if not, cook for another few minutes and then serve.

Chicken Tikka

Servings: 2
Cooking Time:xx
Ingredients:
- 2 chicken breasts, diced
- FIRST MARINADE
- freshly squeezed juice of ½ a lemon
- 1 tablespoon freshly grated ginger
- 1 tablespoon freshly grated garlic
- a good pinch of salt
- SECOND MARINADE
- 100 g/½ cup Greek yogurt
- ½ teaspoon chilli powder
- ½ teaspoon chilli paste
- ½ teaspoon turmeric
- ½ teaspoon garam masala
- 1 tablespoon olive oil

Directions:
1. Mix the ingredients for the first marinade together in a bowl, add in the chicken and stir to coat all the chicken pieces. Leave in the fridge to marinate for 20 minutes.
2. Combine the second marinade ingredients. Once the first marinade has had 20 minutes, add the second marinade to the chicken and stir well. Leave in the fridge for at least 4 hours.
3. Preheat the air-fryer to 180ºC/350ºF.
4. Thread the chicken pieces onto metal skewers that fit in your air-fryer. Add the skewers to the preheated air-fryer and air-fry for 10 minutes. Check the internal temperature of the chicken has reached at least 74ºC/165ºF using a meat thermometer – if not, cook for another few minutes and then serve.

Pepper & Lemon Chicken Wings

Servings: 2
Cooking Time:xx
Ingredients:
- 1kg chicken wings
- 1/4 tsp cayenne pepper
- 2 tsp lemon pepper seasoning
- 3 tbsp butter
- 1 tsp honey
- An extra 1 tsp lemon pepper seasoning for the sauce

Directions:
1. Preheat the air fryer to 260ºC
2. Place the lemon pepper seasoning and cayenne in a bowl and combine
3. Coat the chicken in the seasoning
4. Place the chicken in the air fryer and cook for 20 minutes, turning over halfway
5. Turn the temperature up to 300ºC and cook for another 6 minutes
6. Meanwhile, melt the butter and combine with the honey and the rest of the seasoning
7. Remove the wings from the air fryer and pour the sauce over the top

Air Fryer Bbq Chicken

Servings: 4
Cooking Time:xx
Ingredients:
- 1 whole chicken
- 2 tbsp avocado oil
- 1 tbsp kosher salt
- 1 tsp ground pepper
- 1 tsp garlic powder
- 1 tsp paprika
- ½ tsp dried basil
- ½ tsp dried oregano
- ½ tsp dried thyme

Directions:
1. Mix the seasonings together and spread over chicken
2. Place the chicken in the air fryer breast side down
3. Cook at 182C for 50 minutes and then breast side up for 10 minutes
4. Carve and serve

Turkey Cutlets In Mushroom Sauce

Servings: 2
Cooking Time:xx
Ingredients:
- 2 turkey cutlets
- 1 tbsp butter
- 1 can of cream of mushroom sauce
- 160ml milk
- Salt and pepper for seasoning

Directions:
1. Preheat the air fryer to 220ºC
2. Brush the turkey cults with the butter and seasoning
3. Place in the air fryer and cook for 11 minutes
4. Add the mushroom soup and milk to a pan and cook over the stone for around 10 minutes, stirring every so often
5. Top the turkey cutlets with the sauce

Quick Chicken Nuggets

Servings: 4
Cooking Time:xx
Ingredients:

- 500g chicken tenders
- 25g ranch salad dressing mixture
- 2 tbsp plain flour
- 100g breadcrumbs
- 1 egg, beaten
- Olive oil spray

Directions:

1. Take a large mixing bowl and arrange the chicken inside
2. Sprinkle the seasoning over the top and ensure the chicken is evenly coated
3. Place the chicken to one side for around 10 minutes
4. Add the flour into a resealable bag
5. Crack the egg into a small mixing bowl and whisk
6. Pour the breadcrumbs onto a medium sized plate
7. Transfer the chicken into the resealable bag and coat with the flour, giving it a good shake
8. Remove the chicken and dip into the egg, and then rolling it into the breadcrumbs, coating evenly
9. Repeat with all pieces of the chicken
10. Heat your air fryer to 200°C
11. Arrange the chicken inside the fryer and add a little olive oil spray to avoid sticking
12. Cook for 4 minutes, before turning over and cooking for another 4 minutes
13. Remove and serve whilst hot

Orange Chicken

Servings: 2
Cooking Time:xx
Ingredients:

- 600g chicken thighs, boneless and skinless
- 2 tbsp cornstarch
- 60ml orange juice
- 1 tbsp soy sauce
- 2 tbsp brown sugar
- 1 tbsp rice wine vinegar
- 1/4 teaspoon ground ginger
- Pinch of red pepper flakes
- Zest of one orange
- 2 tsp water and 2 tsp cornstarch mixed together

Directions:

1. Preheat your air fryer to 250°C
2. Take a bowl and combine the chicken with the cornstarch
3. Place in the air fryer and cook for 9 minutes
4. Take a bowl and combine the rest of the ingredients, except for the water and cornstarch mixture
5. Place in a saucepan and bring to the boil and then turn down to a simmer for 5 minutes
6. Add the water and cornstarch mixture to the pan and combine well
7. Remove the chicken from the fryer and pour the sauce over the top

Chicken Milanese

Servings: 4
Cooking Time:xx
Ingredients:

- 130 g/1¾ cups dried breadcrumbs (gluten-free if you wish, see page 9)
- 50 g/⅔ cup grated Parmesan
- 1 teaspoon dried basil
- ½ teaspoon dried thyme
- ¼ teaspoon freshly ground black pepper
- 1 egg, beaten
- 4 tablespoons plain/all-purpose flour (gluten-free if you wish)
- 4 boneless chicken breasts

Directions:

1. Combine the breadcrumbs, cheese, herbs and pepper in a bowl. In a second bowl beat the egg, and in the third bowl have the plain/all-purpose flour. Dip each chicken breast first into the flour, then the egg, then the seasoned breadcrumbs.
2. Preheat the air-fryer to 180°C/350°F.
3. Add the breaded chicken breasts to the preheated air-fryer and air-fry for 12 minutes. Check the internal temperature of the chicken has reached at least 74°C/165°F using a meat thermometer – if not, cook for another few minutes.

Crunchy Chicken Tenders

Servings: 4
Cooking Time:xx
Ingredients:

- 8 regular chicken tenders (frozen work best)
- 1 egg
- 2 tbsp olive oil
- 150g dried breadcrumbs

Directions:

1. Heat the fryer to 175°C
2. In a small bowl, beat the egg
3. In another bowl, combine the oil and the breadcrumbs together
4. Take one tender and first dip it into the egg, and then cover it in the breadcrumb mixture
5. Place the tender into the fryer basket
6. Repeat with the rest of the tenders, arranging them carefully so they don't touch inside the basket
7. Cook for 12 minutes, checking that they are white in the centre before serving

Beef & Lamb And Pork Recipes

Steak Popcorn Bites

Servings: 4
Cooking Time:xx
Ingredients:

- 500g steak, cut into 1" sized cubes
- 500g potato chips, ridged ones work best
- 100g flour
- 2 beaten eggs
- Salt and pepper to taste

Directions:

1. Place the chips into the food processor and pulse unit you get fine chip crumbs
2. Take a bowl and combine the flour with salt and pepper
3. Add the chips to another bowl and the beaten egg to another bowl
4. Take the steak cubes and dip first in the flour, then the egg and then the chip crumbs
5. Preheat your air fryer to 260°C
6. Place the steak pieces into the fryer and cook for 9 minutes

Japanese Pork Chops

Servings: 4
Cooking Time:xx
Ingredients:

- 6 boneless pork chops
- 30g flour
- 2 beaten eggs
- 2 tbsp sweet chilli sauce
- 500g cup seasoned breadcrumbs
- ⅛ tsp salt
- ⅛ tsp pepper
- Tonkatsu sauce to taste

Directions:

1. Place the flour, breadcrumbs and eggs in 3 separate bowls
2. Sprinkle both sides of the pork with salt and pepper
3. Coat the pork in flour, egg and then breadcrumbs
4. Place in the air fryer and cook at 180°C for 8 minutes, turn then cook for a further 5 minutes
5. Serve with sauces on the side

Carne Asada Chips

Servings: 2
Cooking Time:xx
Ingredients:

- 500g sirloin steak
- 1 bag of frozen French fries
- 350g grated cheese
- 2 tbsp sour cream
- 2 tbsp guacamole
- 2 tbsp steak seasoning
- Salt and pepper to taste

Directions:

1. Preheat your oven to 260°C
2. Season the steak with the seasoning and a little salt and pepper
3. Place in the air fryer and cook for 4 minutes, before turning over and cooking for another 4 minutes
4. Remove and allow to rest
5. Add the French fries to the fryer and cook for 5 minutes, shaking regularly
6. Add the cheese
7. Cut the steak into pieces and add on top of the cheese
8. Cook for another 30 seconds, until the cheese is melted
9. Season

Lamb Calzone

Servings: 2
Cooking Time:xx
Ingredients:

- 1 tsp olive oil
- 1 chopped onion
- 100g baby spinach leaves
- 400g minced pork
- 250g whole wheat pizza dough
- 300g grated cheese

Directions:

1. Heat the olive oil in a pan, add the onion and cook for about 2 minutes
2. Add the spinach and cook for a further 1 ½ minutes
3. Stir in marinara sauce and the minced pork
4. Divide the dough into four and roll out into circles
5. Add ¼ of filling to each piece of dough
6. Sprinkle with cheese and fold the dough over to create half moons, crimp edges to seal
7. Spray with cooking spray, place in the air fryer and cook at 160ºC for 12 minutes turning after 8 minutes

Pork Belly With Crackling

Servings: 4
Cooking Time:xx
Ingredients:

- 800g belly pork
- 1 tsp sea salt
- 1 tsp garlic salt
- 2 tsp five spice
- 1 tsp rosemary
- 1 tsp white pepper
- 1 tsp sugar
- Half a lemon

Directions:

1. Cut lines into the meat portion of the belly pork
2. Cook thoroughly in water
3. Allow to air dry for 3 hours
4. Score the skin and prick holes with a fork
5. Rub with the dry rub mix, rub some lemon juice on the skin
6. Place in the air fryer and cook at 160ºC for 30 minutes then at 180ºC for a further 30 minutes

Pork Chops With Honey

Servings: 6
Cooking Time:xx
Ingredients:

- 2 ⅔ tbsp honey
- 100g ketchup
- 6 pork chops
- 2 cloves of garlic
- 2 slices mozzarella cheese

Directions:

1. Preheat air fryer to 200ºC
2. Mix all the ingredients together in a bowl
3. Add the pork chops, allow to marinate for at least 1 hour
4. Place in the air fryer and cook for about 12 minutes turning halfway

Hamburgers

Servings: 4
Cooking Time:xx
Ingredients:
- 500g minced beef
- 1 grated onion
- Salt and pepper to taste

Directions:
1. Preheat air fryer to 200°C
2. Place the grated onion and the beef into a bowl and combine together well
3. Divide minced beef into 4 equal portions, form into patties
4. Season with salt and pepper
5. Place in the air fryer and cook for 10 minutes, turnover and cook for a further 3 minutes

Cheesy Beef Enchiladas

Servings: 4
Cooking Time:xx
Ingredients:
- 500g minced beef
- 1 packet taco seasoning
- 8 tortillas
- 300g grated cheese
- 150g soured cream
- 1 can black beans
- 1 can chopped tomatoes
- 1 can mild chopped chillies
- 1 can red enchilada sauce
- 300g chopped coriander

Directions:
1. Brown the beef and add the taco seasoning
2. Add the beef, beans, tomatoes and chillies to the tortillas
3. Line the air fryer with foil and put the tortillas in
4. Pour the enchilada sauce over the top and sprinkle with cheese
5. Cook at 200°C for five minutes, remove from air fryer add toppings and serve

Tender Ham Steaks

Servings: 1
Cooking Time:xx
Ingredients:
- 1 ham steak
- 2 tbsp brown sugar
- 1 tsp honey
- 2 tbsp melted butter

Directions:
1. Preheat the air fryer to 220°C
2. Combine the melted butter and brown sugar until smooth
3. Add the ham to the air fryer and brush both sides with the butter mixture
4. Cook for 12 minutes, turning halfway through and re-brushing the ham
5. Drizzle honey on top before serving

Old Fashioned Steak

Servings: 4
Cooking Time:xx
Ingredients:
- 4 medium steaks
- 100g flour
- ½ tsp garlic powder
- Salt and pepper
- 1 egg
- 4 slices bacon
- 350ml milk

Directions:
1. Beat the egg
2. Mix the flour with garlic powder, salt and pepper
3. Dip the steak into the egg then cover in the flour mix
4. Place in the air fryer and cook at 170ºC for 7 minutes, turnover and cook for another 10 minutes until golden brown
5. Whilst the steak is cooking, place the bacon in a frying pan, stir in the flour. Add milk to the bacon and stir until there are no lumps in the flour
6. Season with salt and pepper Cook for 2 minutes until thickened season with salt and pepper

Beef And Cheese Empanadas

Servings: 12
Cooking Time:xx
Ingredients:
- 2 tsp oil
- 1 chopped onion
- 1 clove chopped garlic
- 500g minced beef
- Salt and pepper
- 2 tbsp chopped jalapeño
- 2 packs ready made pastry
- 50g grated cheddar cheese
- 50g pepper jack cheese
- 1 egg

Directions:
1. Heat the oil in a pan and fry the onion and garlic until soft
2. Add the meat and jalapeño, season with salt and pepper, and cook until browned
3. Allow the meat to cool
4. Roll out dough as thin as possible and cut into circles, fill with 1 tablespoon of mix, sprinkle with cheese, fold over and seal with the egg
5. Set your fryer to 170ºC and cook for about 12 minutes until golden brown

Mongolian Beef

Servings: 4
Cooking Time:xx
Ingredients:

- 500g steak
- 25g cornstarch
- 2 tsp vegetable oil
- ½ tsp ginger
- 1 tbsp garlic minced
- 75g soy sauce
- 75g water
- 100g brown sugar

Directions:

1. Slice the steak and coat in corn starch
2. Place in the air fryer and cook at 200ºC for 10 minutes turning halfway
3. Place remaining ingredients in a sauce pan and gently warm
4. When cooked place the steak in a bowl and pour the sauce over

Beef Satay

Servings: 2
Cooking Time:xx
Ingredients:

- 400g steak strips
- 2 tbsp oil
- 1 tbsp fish sauce
- 1 tsp sriracha sauce
- 200g sliced coriander (fresh)
- 1 tsp ground coriander
- 1 tbsp soy
- 1 tbsp minced ginger
- 1 tbsp minced garlic
- 1 tbsp sugar
- 25g roasted peanuts

Directions:

1. Add oil, dish sauce, soy, ginger, garlic, sugar sriracha, coriander and ¼ cup coriander to a bowl and mix. Add the steak and marinate for 30 minutes
2. Add the steak to the air fryer and cook at 200ºC for about 8 minutes
3. Place the steak on a plate and top with remaining coriander and chopped peanuts
4. Serve with peanut sauce

Sweet And Sticky Ribs

Servings:2
Cooking Time:1 Hour 15 Minutes
Ingredients:

- 500 g / 17.6 oz pork ribs
- 2 cloves garlic, minced
- 2 tbsp soy sauce
- 2 tsp honey
- 1 tbsp cayenne pepper
- 1 tsp olive oil
- 2 tbsp BBQ sauce
- 1 tsp salt
- 1 tsp black pepper

Directions:

1. Place the pork ribs on a clean surface and cut them into smaller chunks if necessary.
2. In a small mixing bowl, combine the minced garlic, soy sauce, 1 tsp honey, cayenne pepper, olive oil, BBQ sauce, salt, and pepper. Rub the pork ribs into the sauce and spice the mixture until fully coated.
3. Place the coated ribs in the fridge for 1 hour. Meanwhile, preheat the air fryer to 180 °C / 350 °F and line the bottom of the basket with parchment paper.
4. After one hour, transfer the pork ribs into the prepared air fryer basket. Close the lid and cook for 15 minutes, using tongs to turn them halfway through.
5. Once cooked, remove the ribs from the air fryer and use a brush to top each rib with the remaining 1 tsp honey.
6. Return the ribs to the air fryer for a further 2-3 minutes to heat the honey glaze before serving.

Asparagus & Steak Parcels

Servings: 4
Cooking Time:xx
Ingredients:

- 500g flank steak, cut into 6 equal pieces
- 75ml Tamari sauce
- 2 crushed garlic cloves
- 250g trimmed asparagus
- 3 large bell peppers, thinly sliced
- 2 tbsp butter
- Salt and pepper to taste

Directions:

1. Season the steak to your liking
2. Place the meat in a zip top bag and add the Tamari and garlic, sealing the bag closed
3. Make sure the steaks are fully coated in the sauce and leave them in the fright at least 1 hour, but preferably overnight
4. Remove the steaks from the bag and throw the marinade away
5. Place the peppers and sliced asparagus in the centre of each steak piece
6. Roll the steak up and secure in place with a tooth pick
7. Preheat your air fryer to 250ºC
8. Transfer the meat parcels to the air fryer and cook for 5 minutes
9. Allow to rest before serving
10. Melt the butter in a saucepan, over a medium heat, adding the juices from the air fryer
11. Combine well and keep cooking until thickened
12. Pour the sauce over the steak parcels and season to your liking

Sticky Asian Beef

Servings: 2
Cooking Time:xx
Ingredients:

- 1 tbsp coconut oil
- 2 sliced peppers
- 25g liquid aminos
- 25g cup water
- 100g brown sugar
- ¼ tsp pepper
- ½ tsp ground ginger
- ½ tbsp minced garlic
- 1 tsp red pepper flakes
- 600g steak thinly sliced
- ¼ tsp salt

Directions:

1. Melt the coconut oil in a pan, add the peppers and cook until softened
2. In another pan add the aminos, brown sugar, ginger, garlic and pepper flakes. Mix and bring to the boil, simmer for 10 mins
3. Season the steak with salt and pepper
4. Put the steak in the air fryer and cook at 200ºC for 10 minutes. Turn the steak and cook for a further 5 minutes until crispy
5. Add the steak to the peppers then mix with the sauce
6. Serve with rice

Fillet Mignon Wrapped In Bacon

Servings: 2
Cooking Time:xx
Ingredients:

- 1 kg filet mignon
- 500g bacon slices
- Olive oil

Directions:

1. Wrap the fillets in bacon
2. Season with salt and pepper and brush with olive oil
3. Place in the air fryer cook at 200ºC for 9 minutes turning halfway through

Jamaican Jerk Pork

Servings: 4
Cooking Time:xx
Ingredients:
- 400g pork butt cut into 3 pieces
- 100g jerk paste

Directions:
1. Rub the pork with jerk paste and marinate for 4 hours
2. Preheat air fryer to 190ºC
3. Place pork in the air fryer and cook for about 20 minutes turning halfway

Roast Pork

Servings: 4
Cooking Time:xx
Ingredients:
- 500g pork joint
- 1 tbsp olive oil
- 1 tsp salt

Directions:
1. Preheat air fryer to 180ºC
2. Score the pork skin with a knife
3. Drizzle the pork with oil and rub it into the skin, sprinkle with salt
4. Place in the air fryer and cook for about 50 minutes

Southern Style Pork Chops

Servings: 4
Cooking Time:xx
Ingredients:
- 4 pork chops
- 3 tbsp buttermilk
- 100g flour
- Salt and pepper to taste
- Pork rub to taste

Directions:
1. Season the pork with pork rub
2. Drizzle with buttermilk
3. Coat in flour until fully covered
4. Place the pork chops in the air fryer, cook at 170ºC for 15 minutes
5. Turnover and cook for a further 10 minutes

Fish & Seafood Recipes

<u>Air Fryer Mussels</u>

Servings: 2
Cooking Time:xx
Ingredients:

- 400g mussels
- 1 tbsp butter
- 200ml water
- 1 tsp basil
- 2 tsp minced garlic
- 1 tsp chives
- 1 tsp parsley

Directions:

1. Preheat air fryer to 200ºC
2. Clean the mussels, soak for 30 minutes, and remove the beard
3. Add all ingredients to an air fryer-safe pan
4. Cook for 3 minutes
5. Check to see if the mussels have opened, if not cook for a further 2 minutes. Once all mussels are open, they are ready to eat.

<u>Thai Salmon Patties</u>

Servings: 7
Cooking Time:xx
Ingredients:

- 1 large can of salmon, drained and bones removed
- 30g panko breadcrumbs
- ¼ tsp salt
- 1 ½ tbsp Thai red curry paste
- 1 ½ tbsp brown sugar
- Zest of 1 lime
- 2 eggs
- Cooking spray

Directions:

1. Take a large bowl and combine all ingredients together until smooth
2. Use your hands to create patties that are around 1 inch in thickness
3. Preheat your air fryer to 180ºC
4. Coat the patties with cooking spray
5. Cook for 4 minutes each side

<u>Thai Fish Cakes</u>

Servings: 4
Cooking Time:xx
Ingredients:

- 200g pre-mashed potatoes
- 2 fillets of white fish, flaked and mashed
- 1 onion
- 1 tsp butter
- 1 tsp milk
- 1 lime zest and rind
- 3 tsp chilli
- 1 tsp Worcester sauce
- 1 tsp coriander
- 1 tsp mixed spice
- 1 tsp mixed herbs
- 50g breadcrumbs
- Salt and pepper to taste

Directions:

1. Cover the white fish in milk
2. in a mixing bowl place the fish and add the seasoning and mashed potatoes
3. Add the butter and remaining milk
4. Use your hands to create patties and place in the refrigerator for 3 hours
5. Preheat your air fryer to 200ºC
6. Cook for 15 minutes

Sea Bass With Asparagus Spears

Servings: 2
Cooking Time:xx
Ingredients:
- 2 x 100-g/3½-oz. sea bass fillets
- 8 asparagus spears
- 2 teaspoons olive oil
- salt and freshly ground black pepper
- boiled new potatoes, to serve
- CAPER DRESSING
- 1½ tablespoons olive oil
- grated zest and freshly squeezed juice of ½ lemon
- 1 tablespoon small, jarred capers
- 1 teaspoon Dijon mustard
- 1 tablespoon freshly chopped flat-leaf parsley

Directions:
1. Preheat the air-fryer to 180°C/350°F.
2. Prepare the fish and asparagus by brushing both with the olive oil and sprinkling over salt and pepper.
3. Add the asparagus to the preheated air-fryer and air-fry for 4 minutes, then turn the asparagus and add the fish to the air-fryer drawer. Cook for a further 4 minutes. Check the internal temperature of the fish has reached at least 60°C/140°F using a meat thermometer – if not, cook for another minute.
4. Meanwhile, make the dressing by combining all the ingredients in a jar and shaking well. Pour the dressing over the cooked fish and asparagus spears and serve with new potatoes.

Gluten Free Honey And Garlic Shrimp

Servings: 2
Cooking Time:xx
Ingredients:
- 500g fresh shrimp
- 5 tbsp honey
- 2 tbsp gluten free soy sauce
- 2 tbsp tomato ketchup
- 250g frozen stir fry vegetables
- 1 crushed garlic clove
- 1 tsp fresh ginger
- 2 tbsp cornstarch

Directions:
1. Simmer the honey, soy sauce, garlic, tomato ketchup and ginger in a saucepan
2. Add the cornstarch and whisk until sauce thickens
3. Coat the shrimp with the sauce
4. Line the air fryer with foil and add the shrimp and vegetables
5. Cook at 180°C for 10 minutes

Salt & Pepper Calamari

Servings: 2
Cooking Time:xx
Ingredients:

- 500g squid rings
- 500g panko breadcrumbs
- 250g plain flour
- 2 tbsp pepper
- 2 tbsp salt
- 200ml buttermilk
- 1 egg

Directions:

1. Take a medium bowl and combine the buttermilk and egg, stirring well
2. Take another bowl and combine the salt, pepper, flour, and panko breadcrumbs, combining again
3. Dip the quid into the buttermilk first and then the breadcrumbs, coating evenly
4. Place in the air fryer basket
5. Cook at 150°C for 12 minutes, until golden

Traditional Fish And Chips

Servings: 4
Cooking Time:xx
Ingredients:

- 4 potatoes, peeled and cut into chips
- 2 fish fillets of your choice
- 1 beaten egg
- 3 slices of wholemeal bread, grated into breadcrumbs
- 25g tortilla crisps
- 1 lemon rind and juice
- 1 tbsp parsley
- Salt and pepper to taste

Directions:

1. Preheat your air fryer to 200°C
2. Place the chips inside and cook until crispy
3. Cut the fish fillets into 4 slices and season with lemon juice
4. Place the breadcrumbs, lemon rind, parsley, tortillas and seasoning into a food processor and blitz to create a crumb consistency
5. Place the breadcrumbs on a large plate
6. Coat the fish in the egg and then the breadcrumb mixture
7. Cook for 15 minutes at 180°C

Lemon Pepper Shrimp

Servings: 2
Cooking Time:xx
Ingredients:

- ½ tbsp olive oil
- The juice of 1 lemon
- ¼ tsp paprika
- 1 tsp lemon pepper
- ¼ tsp garlic powder
- 400g uncooked shrimp
- 1 sliced lemon

Directions:

1. Preheat air fryer to 200°C
2. Mix olive oil, lemon juice, paprika, lemon pepper and garlic powder. Add the shrimp and mix well
3. Place shrimp in the air fryer and cook for 6-8 minutes until pink and firm.
4. Serve with lemon slices

Pesto Salmon

Servings: 4
Cooking Time:xx
Ingredients:

- 4 x 150–175-g/5½–6-oz. salmon fillets
- lemon wedges, to serve
- PESTO
- 50 g/scant ½ cup toasted pine nuts
- 50 g/2 oz. fresh basil
- 50 g/⅔ cup grated Parmesan or Pecorino
- 100 ml/7 tablespoons olive oil

Directions:

1. To make the pesto, blitz the pine nuts, basil and Parmesan to a paste in a food processor. Pour in the olive oil and process again.
2. Preheat the air-fryer to 160ºC/325ºF.
3. Top each salmon fillet with 2 tablespoons of the pesto. Add the salmon fillets to the preheated air-fryer and air-fry for 9 minutes. Check the internal temperature of the fish has reached at least 63ºC/145ºF using a meat thermometer – if not, cook for another few minutes.

Copycat Fish Fingers

Servings: 2
Cooking Time:xx
Ingredients:

- 2 slices wholemeal bread, grated into breadcrumbs
- 50g plain flour
- 1 beaten egg
- 1 white fish fillet
- The juice of 1 small lemon
- 1 tsp parsley
- 1 tsp thyme
- 1 tsp mixed herbs
- Salt and pepper to taste

Directions:

1. Preheat the air fryer to 180ºC
2. Add salt pepper and parsley to the breadcrumbs and combine well
3. Place the egg in another bowl
4. Place the flour in a separate bowl
5. Place the fish into a food processor and add the lemon juice, salt, pepper thyme and mixed herbs
6. Blitz to create a crumb-like consistency
7. Roll your fish in the flour, then the egg and then the breadcrumbs
8. Cook at 180ºC for 8 minutes

Fish Taco Cauliflower Rice Bowls

Servings: 2
Cooking Time:xx
Ingredients:

- 400g fish of your choice, cut into strips
- 1 tsp chilli powder
- ½ tsp paprika
- 1 sliced avocado
- 25g pickled red onions
- 25g reduced fat sour cream
- ½ tsp cumin
- Salt and pepper to taste
- 300g cauliflower rice
- 1 tbsp lime juice
- 25g fresh coriander
- 1 tbsp sriracha

Directions:

1. Sprinkle both sides of the fish with chilli powder, cumin, paprika, salt and pepper
2. Heat the air fryer to 200ºC, cook the fish for about 12 minutes
3. cook the cauliflower rice according to instructions, mix in lime juice and coriander once cooked
4. Divide the cauliflower rice between two bowls, add the sliced avocado, fish and pickled red onions.
5. Mix the sour cream with the sriracha and drizzle over the top

Garlic Butter Salmon

Servings: 2
Cooking Time:xx
Ingredients:

- 2 salmon fillets, boneless with the skin left on
- 1 tsp minced garlic
- 2 tbsp melted butter
- 1 tsp chopped parsley
- Salt and pepper to taste

Directions:

1. Preheat the air fryer to 270 ºC
2. Take a bowl and combine the melted butter, parsley and garlic to create a sauce
3. Season the salmon to your liking
4. Brush the salmon with the garlic mixture, on both sides
5. Place the salmon into the fryer, with the skin side facing down
6. Cook for 10 minutes - the salmon is done when it flakes with ease

Store-cupboard Fishcakes

Servings: 3
Cooking Time:xx
Ingredients:

- 400 g/14 oz. cooked potato – either mashed potato or the insides of jacket potatoes (see page 124)
- 2 x 150–200-g/5½–7-oz. cans fish, such as tuna or salmon, drained
- 2 eggs
- ¾ teaspoon salt
- 1 teaspoon dried parsley
- ½ teaspoon freshly ground black pepper
- 1 tablespoon olive oil
- caper dressing (see page 79), to serve

Directions:

1. Mix the cooked potato, fish, eggs, salt, parsley and pepper together in a bowl, then divide into 6 equal portions and form into fishcakes. Drizzle the olive oil over both sides of each fishcake.
2. Preheat the air-fryer to 180ºC/350ºF.
3. Add the fishcakes to the preheated air-fryer and air-fry for 15 minutes, turning halfway through cooking. Serve with salad and tartare sauce or Caper Dressing.

Parmesan-coated Fish Fingers

Servings: 2
Cooking Time:xx
Ingredients:

- 350 g/12 oz. cod loins
- 1 tablespoon grated Parmesan
- 40 g/½ cup dried breadcrumbs (gluten-free if you wish, see page 9)
- 1 egg, beaten
- 2 tablespoons plain/all-purpose flour (gluten free if you wish)

Directions:

1. Slice the cod into 6 equal fish fingers/sticks.
2. Mix the Parmesan together with the breadcrumbs. Lay out three bowls: one with flour, one with beaten egg and the other with the Parmesan breadcrumbs. Dip each fish finger/stick first into the flour, then the egg and then the breadcrumbs until fully coated.
3. Preheat the air-fryer to 180ºC/350ºF.
4. Add the fish to the preheated air-fryer and air-fry for 6 minutes. Check the internal temperature of the fish has reached at least 75ºC/167ºF using a meat thermometer – if not, cook for another few minutes. Serve immediately.

Garlic Tilapia

Servings: 2
Cooking Time:xx
Ingredients:

- 2 tilapia fillets
- 2 tsp chopped fresh chives
- 2 tsp chopped fresh parsley
- 2 tsp olive oil
- 1 tsp minced garlic
- Salt and pepper for seasoning

Directions:

1. Preheat the air fryer to 220ºC
2. Take a small bowl and combine the olive oil with the chives, garlic, parsley and a little salt and pepper
3. Brush the mixture over the fish fillets
4. Place the fish into the air fryer and cook for 10 minutes, until flaky

Chilli Lime Tilapia

Servings: 3
Cooking Time:xx
Ingredients:

- 500g Tilapia fillets
- 25g panko crumbs
- 200g flour
- Salt and pepper to taste
- 2 eggs
- 1 tbsp chilli powder
- The juice of 1 lime

Directions:

1. Mix panko, salt and pepper and chilli powder together
2. Whisk the egg in a separate bowl
3. Spray the air fryer with cooking spray
4. Dip the tilapia in the flour, then in the egg and cover in the panko mix
5. Place fish in the air fryer, spray with cooking spray and cook for 7-8 minutes at 190ºC
6. Turn the fish over and cook for a further 7-8 minutes until golden brown.
7. Squeeze lime juice over the top and serve

Air Fryer Tuna

Servings: 2
Cooking Time:xx
Ingredients:

- 2 tuna steaks, boneless and skinless
- 2 tsp honey
- 1 tsp grated ginger
- 4 tbsp soy sauce
- 1 tsp sesame oil
- 1/2 tsp rice vinegar

Directions:

1. Combine the honey, soy sauce, rice vinegar and sesame oil in a bowl until totally mixed together
2. Cover the tuna steaks with the sauce and place in the refrigerator for half an hour to marinade
3. Preheat the air fryer to 270ºC
4. Cook the tuna for 4 minutes
5. Allow to rest before slicing

Crispy Cajun Fish Fingers

Servings: 2
Cooking Time:xx
Ingredients:

- 350 g/12 oz. cod loins
- 1 teaspoon smoked paprika
- ½ teaspoon cayenne pepper
- ½ teaspoon onion granules
- ¾ teaspoon dried oregano
- ¼ teaspoon dried thyme
- ½ teaspoon salt
- ½ teaspoon unrefined sugar
- 40 g/½ cup dried breadcrumbs (gluten-free if you wish, see page 9)
- 2 tablespoons plain/all-purpose flour (gluten-free if you wish)
- 1 egg, beaten

Directions:

1. Slice the cod into 6 equal fish 'fingers'. Mix the spices, herbs, salt and sugar together, then combine with the breadcrumbs. Lay out three bowls: one with flour, one with beaten egg and one with the Cajun-spiced breadcrumbs. Dip each fish finger into the flour, then the egg, then the breadcrumbs until fully coated.
2. Preheat the air-fryer to 180ºC/350ºF.
3. Add the fish to the preheated air-fryer and air-fry for 6 minutes, until cooked inside. Check the internal temperature of the fish has reached at least 75ºC/167ºF using a meat thermometer – if not, cook for another few minutes.

Air Fried Scallops

Servings: 2
Cooking Time:xx
Ingredients:
- 6 scallops
- 1 tbsp olive oil
- Salt and pepper to taste

Directions:
1. Brush the filets with olive oil
2. Sprinkle with salt and pepper
3. Place in the air fryer and cook at 200ºC for 2 mins
4. Turn the scallops over and cook for another 2 minutes

Fish In Foil

Servings: 2
Cooking Time:xx
Ingredients:
- 1 tablespoon avocado oil or olive oil, plus extra for greasing
- 1 tablespoon soy sauce (or tamari)
- 1½ teaspoons freshly grated garlic
- 1½ teaspoons freshly grated ginger
- 1 small red chilli/chile, finely chopped
- 2 skinless, boneless white fish fillets (about 350 g/12 oz. total weight)

Directions:
1. Mix the oil, soy sauce, garlic, ginger and chilli/chile together. Brush a little oil onto two pieces of foil, then lay the fish in the centre of the foil. Spoon the topping mixture over the fish. Wrap the foil around the fish to make a parcel, with a gap above the fish but shallow enough to fit in your air-fryer basket.
2. Preheat the air-fryer to 180ºC/350ºF.
3. Add the foil parcels to the preheated air-fryer and air-fry for 7–10 minutes, depending on the thickness of your fillets. The fish should just flake when a fork is inserted. Serve immediately.

Vegetarian & Vegan Recipes

Aubergine Dip

Servings: 4
Cooking Time:xx
Ingredients:
- 1 aubergine
- 2 tsp oil
- 3 tbsp tahini
- 1 tbsp lemon juice
- 1 clove garlic minced
- ⅛ tsp cumin
- ¼ tsp smoked salt
- ⅛ tsp salt
- Drizzle olive oil

Directions:
1. Cut the aubergine in half length wise and coat in oil, Place in the air fryer and cook at 200°C for 20 minutes
2. Remove from the air fryer and allow to cool
3. Scoop out the aubergine from the peel and put in a food processor
4. Add all the remaining ingredients, blend to combine but not to a puree
5. Serve with a drizzle of olive oil

Artichoke Pasta

Servings: 2
Cooking Time:xx
Ingredients:
- 100g pasta
- 50g basil leaves
- 6 artichoke hearts
- 2 tbsp pumpkin seeds
- 2 tbsp lemon juice
- 1 clove garlic
- ½ tsp white miso paste
- 1 can chickpeas
- 1 tsp olive oil

Directions:
1. Place the chickpeas in the air fryer and cook at 200°C for 12 minutes
2. Cook the pasta according to packet instructions
3. Add the remaining ingredients to a food processor and blend
4. Add the pasta to a bowl and spoon over the pesto mix
5. Serve and top with roasted chickpeas

Air Fryer Cheese Sandwich

Servings:2
Cooking Time:10 Minutes
Ingredients:
- 4 slices white or wholemeal bread
- 2 tbsp butter
- 50 g / 3.5 oz cheddar cheese, grated

Directions:
1. Preheat the air fryer to 180 °C / 350 °F and line the bottom of the basket with parchment paper.
2. Lay the slices of bread out on a clean surface and butter one side of each. Evenly sprinkle the cheese on two of the slices and cover with the final two slices.
3. Transfer the sandwiches to the air fryer, close the lid, and cook for 5 minutes until the bread is crispy and golden, and the cheese is melted.

Pakoras

Servings: 8
Cooking Time:xx
Ingredients:

- 200g chopped cauliflower
- 100g diced pepper
- 250g chickpea flour
- 30ml water
- ½ tsp cumin
- Cooking spray
- 1 onion, diced
- 1 tsp salt
- 1 garlic clove, minced
- 1 tsp curry powder
- 1 tsp coriander
- ½ tsp cayenne

Directions:

1. Preheat air fryer to 175°C
2. Place all ingredients in a bowl and mix well
3. Spray cooking basket with oil
4. Spoon 2 tbsp of mix into the basket and flatten, continue until the basket is full
5. Cook for 8 minutes, turn then cook for a further 8 minutes

Baked Aubergine Slices With Yogurt Dressing

Servings: 2
Cooking Time:xx
Ingredients:

- 1 aubergine/eggplant, sliced 1.5 cm/⅝ in. thick
- 3 tablespoons olive oil
- ½ teaspoon salt
- YOGURT DRESSING
- 1 small garlic clove
- 1 tablespoon tahini or nut butter
- 100 g/½ cup Greek yogurt
- 2 teaspoons freshly squeezed lemon juice
- 1 tablespoon runny honey
- a pinch of salt
- a pinch of ground cumin
- a pinch of sumac
- TO SERVE
- 30 g/1 oz. rocket/arugula
- 2 tablespoons freshly chopped mint
- 3 tablespoons pomegranate seeds

Directions:

1. Preheat the air-fryer to 180°C/350°F.
2. Drizzle the olive oil over each side of the aubergine/eggplant slices. Sprinkle with salt. Add the aubergines to the preheated air-fryer and air-fry for 10 minutes, turning halfway through cooking.
3. Meanwhile, make the dressing by combining all the ingredients in a mini food processor (alterantively, finely chop the garlic, add to a jar with the other ingredients and shake vigorously).
4. Serve the cooked aubergine slices on a bed of rocket/arugula, drizzled with the dressing and with the mint and pomegranate seeds scattered over the top.

Ravioli Air Fryer Style

Servings: 4
Cooking Time:xx

Ingredients:

- Half a pack of frozen ravioli
- 200g Italian breadcrumbs
- 200ml buttermilk
- 5 tbsp marinara sauce
- 1 tbsp olive oil

Directions:

1. Preheat the air fryer to 220°C
2. Place the buttermilk in a bowl
3. Add the breadcrumbs to another bowl
4. Take each piece of ravioli and dip it first into the buttermilk and then into the breadcrumbs, coating evenly
5. Add the ravioli to the air fryer and cook for 7 minutes, adding a small amount of oil at the halfway point
6. Serve with the marinara sauce on the side

Orange Zingy Cauliflower

Servings: 2
Cooking Time:xx

Ingredients:

- 200ml water
- 200g flour
- Half the head of a cauliflower, cut into 1.5" florets
- 2 tsp olive oil
- 2 minced garlic cloves
- 1 tsp minced ginger
- 150ml orange juice
- 3 tbsp white vinegar
- 1/2 tsp red pepper flakes
- 1 tsp sesame oil 100g brown sugar
- 3 tbsp soy sauce
- 1 tbsp cornstarch
- 2 tbsp water
- 1 tsp salt

Directions:

1. Take a medium mixing bowl and add the water, salt and flour together
2. Dip each floret of cauliflower into the mixture and place in the air fryer basket
3. Cook at 220°C for 15 minutes
4. Meanwhile make the orange sauce by combining all ingredients in a saucepan and allowing to simmer for 3 minutes, until the sauce has thickened
5. Drizzle the sauce over the cauliflower to serve

Tofu Bowls

Servings: 4
Cooking Time:xx

Ingredients:

- 1 block of tofu, cut into cubes
- 40ml soy sauce
- 2 tbsp sesame oil
- 1 tsp garlic powder
- 1 chopped onion
- 2 tbsp Tahini dressing
- 3 bunches baby bok choy, chopped
- 300g quinoa
- 1 medium cucumber, sliced
- 1 cup shredded carrot
- 1 avocado, sliced

Directions:

1. Mix the soy sauce, 1 tbsp sesame oil and garlic powder in a bowl. Add the tofu marinade for 10 minutes
2. Place in the air fryer and cook at 200°C for 20 minutes turning halfway
3. Heat the remaining sesame oil in a pan and cook the onions for about 4 minutes
4. Add the bok choy and cook for another 4 minutes
5. Divide the quinoa between your bowls add bok choy, carrot, cucumber and avocado. Top with the tofu and drizzle with Tahini

Roasted Cauliflower

Servings: 2
Cooking Time:xx
Ingredients:
- 3 cloves garlic
- 1 tbsp peanut oil
- ½ tsp salt
- ½ tsp paprika
- 400g cauliflower florets

Directions:
1. Preheat air fryer to 200ºC
2. Crush the garlic, place all ingredients in a bowl and mix well
3. Place in the air fryer and cook for about 15 minutes, shaking every 5 minutes

Crispy Potato Peels

Servings: 1
Cooking Time:xx
Ingredients:
- Peels from 4 potatoes
- Cooking spray
- Salt to season

Directions:
1. Heat the air fryer to 200ºC
2. Place the peels in the air fryer spray with oil and sprinkle with salt
3. Cook for about 6-8 minutes until crispy

Paneer Tikka

Servings: 2
Cooking Time:xx
Ingredients:
- 200ml yogurt
- 1 tsp ginger garlic paste
- 1 tsp red chilli powder
- 1 tsp garam masala
- 1 tsp turmeric powder
- 1 tbsp dried fenugreek leaves
- The juice of 1 lemon
- 2 tbsp chopped coriander
- 1 tbsp olive oil
- 250g paneer cheese, cut into cubes
- 1 green pepper, chopped
- 1 red pepper, chopped
- 1 yellow pepper, chopped
- 1 chopped onion

Directions:
1. Take a mixing bowl and add the yogurt, garlic paste, red chilli powder, garam masala, turmeric powder, lemon juice, fenugreek and chopped coriander, combining well
2. Place the marinade to one side
3. Add the cubed cheese to the marinade and toss to coat well
4. Leave to marinade for 2 hours
5. Take 8 skewers and alternate the cheese with the peppers and onions
6. Drizzle a little oil over the top
7. Arrange in the air fryer and cook at 220ºC for 3 minutes
8. Turn and cook for another 3 minutes

Bbq Sandwich

Servings: 2
Cooking Time:xx
Ingredients:

- 1 tbsp mayo
- ¼ tsp white wine vinegar
- ¼ tsp lemon juice
- 1/8 tsp garlic powder
- Pinch of salt
- Cabbage mix
- 2 sandwich buns
- 150g bbq soy curls

Directions:

1. Mix mayo, white wine vinegar, lemon juice, cabbage mix, garlic powder and pinch of salt to make coleslaw. Set aside
2. Add the buns to the air fryer and cook at 200ºC for 5 minutes to toast
3. Fill the buns with coleslaw, soy curls, pickles and chopped onions

Spanakopita Bites

Servings: 4
Cooking Time:xx
Ingredients:

- 300g baby spinach
- 2 tbsp water
- 100g cottage cheese
- 50g feta cheese
- 2 tbsp grated parmesan
- 1 tbsp olive oil
- 4 sheets of filo pastry
- 1 large egg white
- 1 tsp lemon zest
- 1 tsp oregano
- ¼ tsp salt
- ¼ tsp pepper
- ⅛ tsp cayenne

Directions:

1. Place spinach in water and cook for about 5 minutes, drain
2. Mix all ingredients together
3. Place a sheet of pastry down and brush with oil, place another on the top and do the same, continue until all four on top of each other
4. Ut the pastry into 8 strips then cut each strip in half across the middle
5. Add 1 tbsp of mix to each piece of pastry
6. Fold one corner over the mix to create a triangle, fold over the other corner to seal
7. Place in the air fryer and cook at 190ºC for about 12 minutes until golden brown

Butternut Squash Falafel

Servings: 2
Cooking Time:xx
Ingredients:

- 500 g/1 lb. 2 oz. frozen butternut squash cubes
- 1 tablespoon olive oil, plus extra for cooking
- 100 g/¾ cup canned or cooked chickpeas (drained weight)
- 20 g/¼ cup gram/chickpea flour
- 1 teaspoon ground cumin
- ½ teaspoon ground coriander
- ½ teaspoon salt

Directions:

1. Preheat the air-fryer to 180°C/350°F.
2. Toss the frozen butternut squash in the olive oil. Add to the preheated air-fryer and air-fry for 12–14 minutes, until soft but not caramelized. Remove from the air-fryer and mash the squash by hand or using a food processor, then combine with the chickpeas, flour, spices and salt. Leave the mixture to cool, then divide into 6 equal portions and mould into patties.
3. Preheat the air-fryer to 180°C/350°F.
4. Spray the patties with a little olive oil, then add to the preheated air-fryer and air-fry for 10 minutes, turning once (carefully) during cooking. Enjoy hot or cold.

Two-step Pizza

Servings: 1
Cooking Time:xx
Ingredients:

- BASE
- 130 g/generous ½ cup Greek yogurt
- 125 g self-raising/self-rising flour, plus extra for dusting
- ¼ teaspoon salt
- PIZZA SAUCE
- 100 g/3½ oz. passata/strained tomatoes
- 1 teaspoon dried oregano
- ¼ teaspoon garlic salt
- TOPPINGS
- 75 g/2½ oz. mozzarella, torn
- fresh basil leaves, to garnish

Directions:

1. Mix together the base ingredients in a bowl. Once the mixture starts to look crumbly, use your hands to bring the dough together into a ball. Transfer to a piece of floured parchment paper and roll to about 5 mm/¼ in. thick. Transfer to a second piece of non-floured parchment paper.
2. Preheat the air-fryer to 200°C/400°F.
3. Meanwhile, mix the pizza sauce ingredients together in a small bowl and set aside.
4. Prick the pizza base all over with a fork and transfer (on the parchment paper) to the preheated air-fryer and air-fry for 5 minutes. Turn the pizza base over and top with the pizza sauce and the torn mozzarella. Cook for a further 3–4 minutes, until the cheese has melted. Serve immediately with the basil scattered over the top.

Miso Mushrooms On Sourdough Toast

Servings: 1
Cooking Time:xx
Ingredients:

- 1 teaspoon miso paste
- 1 teaspoon oil, such as avocado or coconut (melted)
- 1 teaspoon soy sauce
- 80 g/3 oz. chestnut mushrooms, sliced 5 mm/½ in. thick
- 1 large slice sourdough bread
- 2 teaspoons butter or plant-based spread
- a little freshly chopped flat-leaf parsley, to serve

Directions:

1. Preheat the air-fryer to 200ºC/400ºF.
2. In a small bowl or ramekin mix together the miso paste, oil and soy sauce.
3. Place the mushrooms in a small shallow gratin dish that fits inside your air-fryer. Add the sauce to the mushrooms and mix together. Place the gratin dish in the preheated air-fryer and air-fry for 6–7 minutes, stirring once during cooking.
4. With 4 minutes left to cook, add the bread to the air-fryer and turn over at 2 minutes whilst giving the mushrooms a final stir.
5. Once cooked, butter the toast and serve the mushrooms on top, scattered with chopped parsley.

Bbq Soy Curls

Servings: 2
Cooking Time:xx
Ingredients:

- 250ml warm water
- 1 tsp vegetable bouillon
- 200g soy curls
- 40g BBQ sauce
- 1 tsp oil

Directions:

1. Soak the soy curls in water and bouillon for 10 minutes
2. Place the soy curls in another bowl and shred
3. Heat the air fryer to 200ºC
4. Cook for 3 minutes
5. Remove from the air fryer and coat in bbq sauce
6. Return to the air fryer and cook for 5 minutes shaking halfway through

Spring Ratatouille

Servings:2
Cooking Time:15 Minutes
Ingredients:

- 1 tbsp olive oil
- 4 Roma tomatoes, sliced
- 2 cloves garlic, minced
- 1 courgette, cut into chunks
- 1 red pepper and 1 yellow pepper, cut into chunks
- 2 tbsp mixed herbs
- 1 tbsp vinegar

Directions:

1. Preheat the air fryer to 190 °C / 370 °F and line the air fryer with parchment paper or grease it with olive oil.
2. Place all of the ingredients into a large mixing bowl and mix until fully combined.
3. Transfer the vegetables into the lined air fryer basket, close the lid, and cook for 15 minutes until the vegetables have softened.

Mini Quiche

Servings: 2
Cooking Time:xx
Ingredients:
- 100g raw cashews
- 3 tbsp milk
- ½ tsp hot sauce
- 1 tsp white miso paste
- 1 tsp mustard
- 300g tofu
- 100g bacon pieces
- 1 chopped red pepper
- 1 chopped onion
- 6 tbsp yeast
- ½ tsp onion powder
- ½ tsp paprika
- ½ tsp cumin
- ½ tsp chilli powder
- ½ tsp black pepper
- ⅛ tsp turmeric
- ½ tsp canola oil
- 50g curly kale

Directions:
1. Heat the oil in a pan, add the bacon pepper, onion and curly kale and cook for about 3 minutes
2. Place all the other ingredients into a blender and blend until smooth
3. Add to a bowl with the bacon, pepper, onion and curly kale and mix well
4. Fill silicone muffin cups with the mix
5. Place in the air fryer and cook at 165°C for 15 minutes

Saganaki

Servings: 2
Cooking Time:xx
Ingredients:
- 200 g/7 oz. kefalotyri or manouri cheese, sliced into wedges 1 cm/½ in. thick
- 2 tablespoons plain/all-purpose flour
- olive oil, for drizzling

Directions:
1. Preheat the air-fryer to 200°C/400°F.
2. Dip each wedge of cheese in the flour, then tap off any excess. Drizzle olive oil onto both sides of the cheese slices
3. Add the cheese to the preheated air-fryer and air-fry for 3 minutes. Remove from the air-fryer and serve.

Side Dishes Recipes

Whole Sweet Potatoes

Servings: 4 As A Side Or Snack
Cooking Time:xx

Ingredients:

- 4 medium sweet potatoes
- 1 tablespoon olive oil
- 1 teaspoon salt
- toppings of your choice

Directions:

1. Preheat the air-fryer to 200ºC/400ºF.
2. Wash and remove any imperfections from the skin of the sweet potatoes, then rub the potatoes with the olive oil and salt.
3. Add the sweet potatoes to the preheated air-fryer and air-fry for up to 40 minutes (the cooking time depends on the size of the potatoes). Remove as soon as they are soft when pierced. Slice open and serve with your choice of toppings.
4. VARIATION: WHOLE JACKET POTATOES
5. Regular baking potatoes can be air-fried in the same way, but will require a cooking time of 45–60 minutes, depending on their size.

Sweet Potato Tots

Servings: 24
Cooking Time:xx

Ingredients:

- 2 sweet potatoes, peeled
- ½ tsp cajun seasoning
- Olive oil cooking spray
- Sea salt to taste

Directions:

1. Boil the sweet potatoes in a pan for about 15 minutes, allow to cool
2. Grate the sweet potato and mix in the cajun seasoning
3. Form into tot shaped cylinders
4. Spray the air fryer with oil, place the tots in the air fryer
5. Sprinkle with salt and cook for 8 minutes at 200ºC, turn and cook for another 8 minutes

Ricotta Stuffed Aubergine

Servings: 2
Cooking Time:xx

Ingredients:

- 1 aubergine
- 150g ricotta cheese
- 75g Parmesan cheese, plus an extra 75g for the breading
- 1 tsp garlic powder
- 3 tbsp parsley
- 1 egg, plus an extra 2 eggs for the breading
- 300g pork rind crumbs
- 2 tsp Italian seasoning

Directions:

1. Cut the aubergine into rounds, about 1/2" in thickness
2. Line a baking sheet with parchment and arrange the rounds on top, sprinkling with salt
3. Place another sheet of parchment on top and place something heavy on top to get rid of excess water
4. Leave for 30 minutes
5. Take a bowl and combine the egg, ricotta, 75g Parmesan and parsley, until smooth
6. Remove the parchment from the aubergine and wipe off the salt
7. Take a tablespoon of the ricotta mixture and place on top of each round of aubergine, spreading with a knife
8. Place in the freezer for a while to set
9. Take a bowl and add the two eggs, the pork rinds, parmesan and seasonings, and combine
10. Remove the aubergine from the freezer and coat each one in the mixture completely
11. Place back in the freezer for 45 minutes
12. Cook in the air fryer for 8 minutes at 250ºC

Grilled Bacon And Cheese

Servings: 2
Cooking Time:xx
Ingredients:

- 4 slices of regular bread
- 1 tbsp butter
- 2 slices cheddar cheese
- 5 slices bacon, pre-cooked
- 2 slices mozzarella cheese

Directions:

1. Place the butter into the microwave to melt
2. Spread the butter onto one side of the bread slices
3. Place one slice of bread into the fryer basket, with the buttered side facing downwards
4. Place the cheddar on top, followed by the bacon, mozzarella and the other slice of bread, with the buttered side facing upwards
5. Set your fryer to 170ºC and cook the sandwich for 4 minutes
6. Turn the sandwich over and cook for another 3 minutes
7. Turn the sandwich out and serve whilst hot
8. Repeat with the other remaining sandwich

Bbq Beetroot Crisps

Servings:4
Cooking Time:5 Minutes
Ingredients:

- 400 g / 14 oz beetroot, sliced
- 2 tbsp olive oil
- 1 tbsp BBQ seasoning
- ½ tsp black pepper

Directions:

1. Preheat the air fryer to 180 °C / 350 °F and line the bottom of the basket with parchment paper.
2. Place the beetroot slices in a large bowl. Add the olive oil, BBQ seasoning, and black pepper, and toss to coat the beetroot slices on both sides.
3. Place the beetroot slices in the air fryer and cook for 5 minutes until hot and crispy.

Cauliflower With Hot Sauce And Blue Cheese Sauce

Servings:2
Cooking Time:15 Minutes
Ingredients:

- For the cauliflower:
- 1 cauliflower, broken into florets
- 4 tbsp hot sauce
- 2 tbsp olive oil
- 1 tsp garlic powder
- ½ tsp salt
- ½ tsp black pepper
- 1 tbsp plain flour
- 1 tbsp corn starch
- For the blue cheese sauce:
- 50 g / 1.8 oz blue cheese, crumbled
- 2 tbsp sour cream
- 2 tbsp mayonnaise
- ½ tsp salt
- ½ tsp black pepper

Directions:

1. Preheat the air fryer to 180 °C / 350 °F and line the bottom of the basket with parchment paper.
2. In a bowl, combine the hot sauce, olive oil, garlic powder, salt, and black pepper until it forms a consistent mixture. Add the cauliflower to the bowl and coat in the sauce.
3. Stir in the plain flour and corn starch until well combined.
4. Transfer the cauliflower to the lined basket in the air fryer, close the lid, and cook for 12-15 minutes until the cauliflower has softened and is golden in colour.
5. Meanwhile, make the blue cheese sauce by combining all of the ingredients. When the cauliflower is ready, remove it from the air fryer and serve with the blue cheese sauce on the side.

Mexican Rice

Servings: 4
Cooking Time:xx
Ingredients:

- 500g long grain rice
- 3 tbsp olive oil
- 60ml water
- 1 tsp chilli powder
- 1/4 tsp cumin
- 2 tbsp tomato paste
- 1/2 tsp garlic powder
- 1tsp red pepper flakes
- 1 chopped onion
- 500ml chicken stock
- Half a small jalapeño pepper with seeds out, chopped
- Salt for seasoning

Directions:

1. Add the water and tomato paste and combine, placing to one side
2. Take a baking pan and add a little oil
3. Wash the rice and add to the baking pan
4. Add the chicken stock, tomato paste, jalapeños, onions, and the rest of the olive oil, and combine
5. Place aluminium foil over the top and place in your air fryer
6. Cook at 220ºC for 50 minutes
7. Keep checking the rice as it cooks, as the liquid should be absorbing

Asparagus Spears

Servings: 2
Cooking Time:xx
Ingredients:

- 1 bunch of trimmed asparagus
- 1 teaspoon olive oil
- ¼ teaspoon salt
- ⅛ teaspoon freshly ground black pepper

Directions:

1. Preheat the air-fryer to 180ºC/350ºF.
2. Toss the asparagus spears in the oil and seasoning. Add these to the preheated air-fryer and air-fry for 8–12 minutes, turning once (cooking time depends on the thickness of the stalks, which should retain some bite).

Super Easy Fries

Servings: 2
Cooking Time:xx
Ingredients:

- 500g potatoes cut into ½ inch sticks
- 1 tsp olive oil
- ¼ tsp salt
- ¼ tsp pepper

Directions:

1. Place the potatoes in a bowl cover with water and allow to soak for 30 minutes
2. Spread the butter onto one side of the bread slices
3. Pat dry with paper, drizzle with oil and toss to coat
4. Place in the air fryer and cook at 200ºC for about 15 minutes, keep tossing through cooking time
5. Sprinkle with salt and pepper

Celery Root Fries

Servings: 2
Cooking Time:xx
Ingredients:

- ½ celeriac, cut into sticks
- 500ml water
- 1 tbsp lime juice
- 1 tbsp olive oil
- 75g mayo
- 1 tbsp mustard
- 1 tbsp powdered horseradish

Directions:

1. Put celeriac in a bowl, add water and lime juice, soak for 30 minutes
2. Preheat air fryer to 200
3. Mix together the mayo, horseradish powder and mustard, refrigerate
4. Drain the celeriac, drizzle with oil and season with salt and pepper
5. Place in the air fryer and cook for about 10 minutes turning halfway
6. Serve with the mayo mix as a dip

Roasted Okra

Servings: 1
Cooking Time:xx
Ingredients:

- 300g Okra, ends trimmed and pods sliced
- 1 tsp olive oil
- ¼ tsp salt
- ⅛ tsp pepper

Directions:

1. Preheat the air fryer to 175°C
2. Combine all ingredients in a bowl and stir gently
3. Place in the air fryer and cook for 5 minutes, shake and cook for another 5 minutes

Sweet & Spicy Baby Peppers

Servings: 2
Cooking Time:xx
Ingredients:

- 200 g/7 oz. piccarella (baby) peppers, deseeded and quartered lengthways
- 1 teaspoon olive oil
- ½ teaspoon chilli/chili paste
- ¼ teaspoon runny honey
- salt and freshly ground black pepper

Directions:

1. Preheat the air-fryer to 180°C/350°F.
2. Toss the peppers in the oil, chilli/chili paste and honey, then add salt and pepper to taste.
3. Place in the preheated air-fryer and air-fry for 6–8 minutes, depending on how 'chargrilled' you like them, turning them over halfway through.

Asparagus Fries

Servings: 2
Cooking Time:xx
Ingredients:

- 1 egg
- 1 tsp honey
- 100g panko bread crumbs
- Pinch of cayenne pepper
- 100g grated parmesan
- 12 asparagus spears
- 75g mustard
- 75g Greek yogurt

Directions:

1. Preheat air fryer to 200°C
2. Combine egg and honey in a bowl, mix panko crumbs and parmesan on a plate
3. Coat each asparagus in egg then in the bread crumbs
4. Place in the air fryer and cook for about 6 mins
5. Mix the remaining ingredients in a bowl and serve as a dipping sauce

Orange Tofu

Servings: 4
Cooking Time:xx
Ingredients:

- 400g tofu, drained
- 1 tbsp tamari
- 1 tbsp corn starch
- ¼ tsp pepper flakes
- 1 tsp minced ginger
- 1 tsp fresh garlic
- 1 tsp orange zest
- 75ml orange juice
- 75ml water
- 2 tsp cornstarch
- 1 tbsp maple syrup

Directions:

1. Cut the tofu into cubes, place in a bowl add the tamari and mix well
2. Mix in 1 tbsp starch and allow to marinate for 30 minutes
3. Place the remaining ingredients into another bowl and mix well
4. Place the tofu in the air fryer and cook at 190°C for about 10 minutes
5. Add tofu to a pan with sauce mix and cook until sauce thickens

Mediterranean Vegetables

Servings: 1–2
Cooking Time:xx
Ingredients:

- 1 courgette/zucchini, thickly sliced
- 1 (bell) pepper, deseeded and chopped into large chunks
- 1 red onion, sliced into wedges
- 12 cherry tomatoes
- 1 tablespoon olive oil
- ½ teaspoon salt
- ½ teaspoon freshly ground black pepper
- 2 rosemary twigs
- mozzarella, fresh pesto (see page 80) and basil leaves, to serve

Directions:

1. Preheat the air-fryer to 180°C/350°F.
2. Toss the prepared vegetables in the oil and seasoning. Add the vegetables and the rosemary to the preheated air-fryer and air-fry for 12–14 minutes, depending on how 'chargrilled' you like them.
3. Remove and serve topped with fresh mozzarella and pesto and scattered with basil leaves.

Butternut Squash Fries

Servings: 4
Cooking Time:xx
Ingredients:
- 400g butternut squash, cut into sticks
- 1 tbsp olive oil
- 2 tbsp bagel seasoning
- 1 tsp fresh chopped rosemary

Directions:
1. Preheat air fryer to 200°C
2. Drizzle butternut squash with olive oil mix to coat
3. Add to the air fryer, cook for about 22 minutes until golden brown, stirring every 4 minutes
4. Sprinkle with bagel seasoning to serve

Potato Wedges With Rosemary

Servings: 2
Cooking Time:xx
Ingredients:
- 2 potatoes, sliced into wedges
- 1 tbsp olive oil
- 2 tsp seasoned salt
- 2 tbsp chopped rosemary

Directions:
1. Preheat air fryer to 190°C
2. Drizzle potatoes with oil, mix in salt and rosemary
3. Place in the air fryer and cook for 20 minutes turning halfway

Air Fryer Eggy Bread

Servings:2
Cooking Time:5-7 Minutes
Ingredients:
- 4 slices white bread
- 4 eggs, beaten
- 1 tsp black pepper
- 1 tsp dried chives

Directions:
1. Preheat your air fryer to 150 °C / 300 °F and line the bottom of the basket with parchment paper.
2. Whisk the eggs in a large mixing bowl and soak each slice of bread until fully coated.
3. Transfer the eggy bread to the preheated air fryer and cook for 5-7 minutes until the eggs are set and the bread is crispy.
4. Serve hot with a sprinkle of black pepper and chives on top.

Hasselback New Potatoes

Servings: 4
Cooking Time:xx
Ingredients:

- 8–12 new potatoes, roughly 5–7 cm/2–2¾ in. in length
- 2 teaspoons olive oil
- salt
- 1 tablespoon butter (optional)

Directions:

1. Preheat the air-fryer to 180ºC/350ºF.
2. Slice the potatoes multiple times widthways, making sure you do not cut all the way through (if you place the potatoes in the bowl of a wooden spoon to make these slices, it prevents you cutting all the way through). Coat the potatoes in the olive oil and sprinkle over the salt.
3. Add the potatoes to the preheated air-fryer and air-fry for 20–25 minutes until the potatoes are crispy on the outside but soft on the inside. Serve immediately.

Sweet Potato Wedges

Servings:4
Cooking Time:20 Minutes
Ingredients:

- ½ tsp garlic powder
- ½ tsp cumin
- ½ tsp smoked paprika
- ½ tsp cayenne pepper
- ½ tsp salt
- ½ tsp black pepper
- 1 tsp dried chives
- 4 tbsp olive oil
- 3 large sweet potatoes, cut into wedges

Directions:

1. Preheat the air fryer to 180 °C / 350 °F and line the bottom of the basket with parchment paper.
2. In a bowl, mix the garlic powder, cumin, smoked paprika, cayenne pepper, salt, black pepper, and dried chives until combined.
3. Whisk in the olive oil and coat the sweet potato wedges in the spicy oil mixture.
4. Transfer the coated sweet potatoes to the air fryer and close the lid. Cook for 20 minutes until cooked and crispy. Serve hot as a side with your main meal.

Desserts Recipes

Fruit Crumble

Servings: 2
Cooking Time:xx
Ingredients:
- 1 diced apple
- 75g frozen blackberries
- 25g brown rice flour
- 2 tbsp sugar
- ½ tsp cinnamon
- 2 tbsp butter

Directions:
1. Preheat air fryer to 150°C
2. Mix apple and blackberries in an air fryer safe baking pan
3. In a bowl mix the flour, sugar, cinnamon and butter, spoon over the fruit
4. Cook for 15 minutes

Chocolate-glazed Banana Slices

Servings:2
Cooking Time:10 Minutes
Ingredients:
- 2 bananas
- 1 tbsp honey
- 1 tbsp chocolate spread, melted
- 2 tbsp milk chocolate chips

Directions:
1. Preheat the air fryer to 180 °C / 350 °F. Remove the mesh basket from the machine and line it with parchment paper.
2. Cut the two bananas into even slices and place them in the lined air fryer basket.
3. In a small bowl, mix the honey and melted chocolate spread. Use a brush to glaze the banana slices. Carefully press the milk chocolate chips into the banana slices enough so that they won't fall out when you transfer the bananas into the air fryer.
4. Carefully slide the mesh basket into the air fryer, close the lid, and cook for 10 minutes until the bananas are hot and the choc chips have melted.
5. Enjoy the banana slices on their own or with a side of ice cream.

Apple And Cinnamon Empanadas

Servings: 12
Cooking Time:xx
Ingredients:
- 12 empanada wraps
- 2 diced apples
- 2 tbsp honey
- 1 tsp vanilla extract
- 1 tsp cinnamon
- ⅛ tsp nutmeg
- Olive oil spray
- 2 tsp cornstarch
- 1 tsp water

Directions:
1. Place apples, cinnamon, honey, vanilla and nutmeg in a pan cook for 2-3 minutes until apples are soft
2. Mix the cornstarch and water add to the pan and cook for 30 seconds
3. Add the apple mix to each of the empanada wraps
4. Roll the wrap in half, pinch along the edges, fold the edges in then continue to roll to seal
5. Place in the air fryer and cook at 200°C for 8 minutes, turn and cook for another 10 minutes

Butter Cake

Servings: 4
Cooking Time:xx
Ingredients:

- Cooking spray
- 7 tbsp butter
- 25g white sugar
- 2 tbsp white sugar
- 1 egg
- 300g flour
- Pinch salt
- 6 tbsp milk

Directions:

1. Preheat air fryer to 175ºC
2. Spray a small fluted tube pan with cooking spray
3. Beat the butter and all of the sugar together in a bowl until creamy
4. Add the egg and mix until fluffy, add the salt and flour mix well. Add the milk and mix well
5. Put the mix in the pan and cook in the air fryer for 15 minutes

French Toast Sticks

Servings: 12
Cooking Time:xx
Ingredients:

- 2 eggs
- 25g milk
- 1 tbsp melted butter
- 1 tsp vanilla extract
- 1 tsp cinnamon
- 4 slices bread, cut into thirds
- 1 tsp icing sugar

Directions:

1. Mix eggs, milk, butter, vanilla and cinnamon together in a bowl
2. Line the air fryer with parchment paper
3. Dip each piece of bread into the egg mixture
4. Place in the air fryer and cook at 190ºC for 6 minutes, turn over and cook for another 3 minutes
5. Sprinkle with icing sugar to serve

Key Lime Cupcakes

Servings: 6
Cooking Time:xx
Ingredients:

- 250g Greek yogurt
- 200g soft cheese
- 2 eggs
- Juice and rind of 2 limes
- 1 egg yolk
- ¼ cup caster sugar
- 1 tsp vanilla essence

Directions:

1. Mix the Greek yogurt and soft cheese together until smooth
2. Add the eggs and mix, add the lime juice, rind, vanilla and caster sugar and mix well
3. Fill 6 cupcake cases with the mix and place the rest to one side
4. Place in the air fryer and cook at 160ºC for 10 minutes then another 10 minutes at 180ºC
5. Place the remaining mix into a piping bag, once the cupcakes have cooled pipe on the top and place in the fridge to set

Chonut Holes

Servings: 12
Cooking Time:xx
Ingredients:

- 225g flour
- 75g sugar
- 1 tsp baking powder
- ¼ tsp cinnamon
- 2 tbsp sugar

- ½ tsp salt
- 2 tbsp aquafaba
- 1 tbsp melted coconut oil
- 75ml soy milk
- 2 tsp cinnamon

Directions:

1. In a bowl mix the flour, ¼ cup sugar, baking powder, ¼ tsp cinnamon and salt
2. Add the aquafaba, coconut oil and soy milk mix well
3. In another bowl mix 2 tsp cinnamon and 2 tbsp sugar
4. Line the air fryer with parchment paper
5. Divide the dough into 12 pieces and dredge with the cinnamon sugar mix
6. Place in the air fryer at 185ºC and cook for 6-8 minutes, don't shake them

Peanut Butter & Chocolate Baked Oats

Servings:9
Cooking Time:xx
Ingredients:

- 150 g/1 heaped cup rolled oats/quick-cooking oats
- 50 g/⅓ cup dark chocolate chips or buttons
- 300 ml/1¼ cups milk or plant-based milk
- 50 g/3½ tablespoons Greek or plant-based yogurt
- 1 tablespoon runny honey or maple syrup
- ½ teaspoon ground cinnamon or ground ginger
- 65 g/scant ⅓ cup smooth peanut butter

Directions:

1. Stir all the ingredients together in a bowl, then transfer to a baking dish that fits your air-fryer drawer.
2. Preheat the air-fryer to 180ºC/350ºF.
3. Add the baking dish to the preheated air-fryer and air-fry for 10 minutes. Remove from the air-fryer and serve hot, cut into 9 squares.

Special Oreos

Servings: 9
Cooking Time:xx
Ingredients:

- 100g pancake mix
- 25ml water
- Cooking spray
- 9 Oreos
- 1 tbsp icing sugar

Directions:

1. Mix pancake mix and water until well combined
2. Line the air fryer with parchment paper and spray with cooking spray
3. Preheat the air fryer to 200ºC
4. Dip each cookie in the pancake mix and place in the air fryer
5. Cook for 5 minutes, turn and cook for a further 3 minutes
6. Sprinkle with icing sugar to serve

Chocolate Orange Muffins

Servings: 12
Cooking Time:xx
Ingredients:
- 100g self raising flour
- 110g caster sugar
- 50g butter
- 20g cocoa powder
- 50ml milk
- 1 tsp cocoa nibs
- 1 large orange juice and rind
- 1 tbsp honey
- 1tsp vanilla essence
- 2 eggs

Directions:
1. Add the flour, butter and sugar to a mixing bowl and rug together
2. Add the cocoa, honey, orange and vanilla mix well
3. Mix the milk and egg together then add to the flour mix, combine well
4. Rub your muffin cases with flour to stop them sticking, add 2 tbsp batter to each one
5. Cook in the air fryer for 12 minutes at 180ºC

Chocolate Dipped Biscuits

Servings: 6
Cooking Time:xx
Ingredients:
- 225g self raising flour
- 100g sugar
- 100g butter
- 50g milk chocolate
- 1 egg beaten
- 1 tsp vanilla essence

Directions:
1. Add the flour, butter and sugar to a bowl and rub together
2. Add the egg and vanilla, mix to form a dough
3. Split the dough into 6 and form into balls
4. Place in the air fryer cook at 180ºC for 15 minutes
5. Melt the chocolate, dip the cooked biscuits into the chocolate and half cover

Pistachio Brownies

Servings: 4
Cooking Time:xx
Ingredients:
- 75ml milk
- ½ tsp vanilla extract
- 25g salt
- 25g pecans
- 75g flour
- 75g sugar
- 25g cocoa powder
- 1 tbsp ground flax seeds

Directions:
1. Mix all of the dry ingredients together, in another bowl mix the wet ingredients
2. Add all the ingredients together and mix well
3. Preheat the air fryer to 175ºC
4. Line a 5 inch cake tin with parchment paper
5. Pour the brownie mix into the cake tin and cook in the air fryer for about 20 minutes

Pecan & Molasses Flapjack

Servings:9
Cooking Time:xx
Ingredients:

- 120 g/½ cup plus 2 teaspoons butter or plant-based spread, plus extra for greasing
- 40 g/2 tablespoons blackstrap molasses
- 60 g/5 tablespoons unrefined sugar
- 50 g/½ cup chopped pecans
- 200 g/1½ cups porridge oats/steelcut oats (not rolled or jumbo)

Directions:

1. Preheat the air-fryer to 180ºC/350ºF.
2. Grease and line a 15 x 15-cm/6 x 6-in. baking pan.
3. In a large saucepan melt the butter/spread, molasses and sugar. Once melted, stir in the pecans, then the oats. As soon as they are combined, tip the mixture into the prepared baking pan and cover with foil.
4. Place the foil-covered baking pan in the preheated air-fryer and air-fry for 10 minutes. Remove the foil, then cook for a further 2 minutes to brown the top. Leave to cool, then cut into 9 squares.

Peanut Butter And Banana Bites

Servings: 12
Cooking Time:xx
Ingredients:

- 1 banana
- 12 wonton wrappers
- 75g peanut butter
- 1-2 tsp vegetable oil

Directions:

1. Slice the banana and place in a bowl of water with lemon juice to prevent browning
2. Place one piece of banana and a spoon of peanut butter in each wonton wrapper
3. Wet the edges of each wrapper and fold over to seal
4. Spray the air fryer with oil
5. Place in the air fryer and cook at 190ºC for 6 minutes

Apple And Cinnamon Puff Pastry Pies

Servings:8
Cooking Time:20 Minutes
Ingredients:

- 4 tbsp butter
- 4 tbsp white sugar
- 2 tbsp brown sugar
- 1 tsp cinnamon
- 1 tsp nutmeg
- 1 tsp salt
- 4 apples, peeled and diced
- 2 large sheets puff pastry
- 1 egg

Directions:

1. Preheat the air fryer to 180 °C / 350 °F. Remove the mesh basket from the machine and line it with parchment paper.
2. In a bowl, whisk together the butter, white sugar, brown sugar, cinnamon, nutmeg, and salt.
3. Place the apples in a heatproof baking dish and coat them in the butter and sugar mixture. Transfer to the air fryer and cook for 10 minutes.
4. Meanwhile, roll out the pastry on a clean, floured surface. Cut the sheets into 8 equal parts.
5. Once the apples are hot and softened, evenly spread the mixture between the pastry sheets. Fold the sheets over to cover the apple and gently press the edges using a fork or your fingers to seal the mixture in.
6. Beat the egg in a bowl and use a brush to coat the top of each pastry sheet.
7. Carefully transfer the filled pastry sheets to the prepared air fryer basket, close the lid, and cook for 10 minutes until the pastry is golden and crispy.

Tasty Cannoli

Servings: 4
Cooking Time:xx

Ingredients:

- 400g ricotta cheese
- 200g mascarpone cheese
- 150g icing sugar
- 160ml double cream
- 1 tsp vanilla extract
- 1 tsp orange zest
- 150g mini chocolate chips
- 350g flour
- 150g sugar
- 1 tsp salt
- 1/2 tsp cinnamon
- 6 tbsp white wine
- 1 egg, plus 1 extra egg white
- 4 tbsp cubed cold butter

Directions:

1. Take a large mixing bowl and a hand mixer. Combine the cream and half the icing sugar until you see stiff peaks starting to form
2. Take another bowl and combine the rest of the icing sugar with the ricotta, mascarpone, zest, salt and vanilla
3. Fold the ricotta mixture into the cream mixture carefully and place in the refrigerator for 1 hour
4. Take a large bowl and combine the cinnamon, salt, sugar and lour
5. Cut the butter into chunks and add to the mixture, combining well
6. Add the egg and the wine and combine until you see a dough starting to form
7. Cover the dough with plastic wrap and place in the refrigerator for 1 hour
8. Cut the dough into halves and roll each half into about 1/8" thickness
9. Use a cookie cutter (around 4" size) to cut out rounds
10. Wrap the cold dough around your cannoli moulds
11. Brush the seal with the egg white to hold it together
12. Preheat the air fryer to 220°C
13. Place the cannoli in the basket and cook for 12 minutes
14. Once cooled slightly, remove the moulds
15. Place the cream mixture into a pastry bag and pipe into the cannoli shells
16. Dip both ends into the chocolate chips for decoration

Grain-free Millionaire's Shortbread

Servings:9
Cooking Time:xx

Ingredients:

- BASE
- 60 g/5 tablespoons coconut oil
- 1 tablespoon maple syrup
- ½ teaspoon vanilla extract
- 180 g/1¾ cups ground almonds
- a pinch of salt
- MIDDLE
- 185 g/1⅓ cups dried pitted dates (soak in hot water for at least 20 minutes, then drain)
- 2 tablespoons almond butter
- 90 g/scant ½ cup canned coconut milk (the thick part once it has separated is ideal)
- TOPPING
- 125 g/½ cup coconut oil
- 4 tablespoons cacao powder
- 1 tablespoon maple syrup

Directions:

1. Preheat the air-fryer to 180°C/350°F.
2. To make the base, in a small saucepan melt the coconut oil with the maple syrup and vanilla extract. As soon as the coconut oil is melted, stir in the almonds and the salt off the heat. Press this mixture into a 15 x 15-cm/6 x 6-in. baking pan.
3. Add the baking pan to the preheated air-fryer and cook for 4 minutes, until golden brown on top. Remove from the air-fryer and allow to cool.
4. In a food processor, combine the rehydrated drained dates, almond butter and coconut milk. Once the base is cool, pour this mixture over the base and pop into the freezer to set for an hour.
5. After the base has had 45 minutes in the freezer, make the topping by heating the coconut oil in a saucepan until melted, then whisk in the cacao powder and maple syrup off the heat to make a chocolate syrup. Leave this to cool for 15 minutes, then pour over the set middle layer and return to the freezer for 30 minutes. Cut into 9 squares to serve.

Thai Fried Bananas

Servings: 8
Cooking Time:xx
Ingredients:

- 4 ripe bananas
- 2 tbsp flour
- 2 tbsp rice flour
- 2 tbsp cornflour
- 2 tbsp desiccated coconut
- Pinch salt
- ½ tsp baking powder
- ½ tsp cardamon powder

Directions:

1. Place all the dry ingredients in a bowl and mix well. Add a little water at a time and combine to form a batter
2. Cut the bananas in half and then half again length wise
3. Line the air fryer with parchment paper and spray with cooking spray
4. Dip each banana piece in the batter mix and place in the air fryer
5. Cook at 200ºC for 10 -15 minutes turning halfway
6. Serve with ice cream

Peach Pies

Servings: 8
Cooking Time:xx
Ingredients:

- 2 peaches, peeled and chopped
- 1 tbsp lemon juice
- 3 tbsp sugar
- 1 tsp vanilla extract
- ¼ tsp salt
- 1 tsp cornstarch
- 1 pack ready made pastry
- Cooking spray

Directions:

1. Mix together peaches, lemon juice, sugar and vanilla in a bowl. Stand for 15 minutes
2. Drain the peaches keeping 1 tbsp of the liquid, mix cornstarch into the peaches
3. Cut the pastry into 8 circles, fill with the peach mix
4. Brush the edges of the pastry with water and fold over to form half moons, crimp the edges to seal
5. Coat with cooking spray
6. Add to the air fryer and cook at 170ºC for 12 minutes until golden brown

Milk And White Chocolate Chip Air Fryer Donuts With Frosting

Servings:4

Cooking Time:10 Minutes

Ingredients:

- For the donuts:
- 200 ml milk (any kind)
- 50 g / 3.5 oz brown sugar
- 50 g / 3.5 oz granulated sugar
- 1 tbsp active dry yeast
- 2 tbsp olive oil
- 4 tbsp butter, melted
- 1 egg, beaten
- 1 tsp vanilla extract
- 400 g / 14 oz plain flour
- 4 tbsp cocoa powder
- 100 g / 3.5 oz milk chocolate chips
- For the frosting:
- 5 tbsp powdered sugar
- 2 tbsp cocoa powder
- 100 ml heavy cream
- 50 g / 1.8 oz white chocolate chips, melted

Directions:

1. To make the donuts, whisk together the milk, brown and granulated sugars, and active dry yeast in a bowl. Set aside for a few minutes while the yeast starts to get foamy.

2. Stir the melted butter, beaten egg, and vanilla extract into the bowl. Mix well until all of the ingredients are combined.

3. Fold in the plain flour and cocoa powder until a smooth mixture forms.

4. Lightly flour a clean kitchen top surface and roll the dough out. Gently knead the dough for 2-3 minutes until it becomes soft and slightly tacky.

5. Transfer the dough into a large mixing bowl and cover it with a clean tea towel or some tinfoil. Leave the dough to rise for around one hour in a warm place.

6. Remove the tea towel or tinfoil from the bowl and roll it out on a floured surface once again. Use a rolling pin to roll the dough into a one-inch thick circle.

7. Use a round cookie cutter to create circular donuts and place each one into a lined air fryer basket.

8. Once all of the donuts have been placed into the air fryer, turn the machine onto 150 °C / 300 °F and close the lid.

9. Cook the donuts for 8-10 minutes until they are slightly golden and crispy on the outside.

10. While the donuts are cooking in the air fryer, make the frosting by combining the powdered sugar, cocoa powder, heavy cream, and melted white chocolate chips in a bowl. Mix well until a smooth, sticky mixture forms.

11. When the donuts are cooked, remove them from the air fryer and set aside to cool for 5-10 minutes. Once cooled, evenly spread some frosting on the top layer of each one. Place in the fridge to set for at least one hour.

12. Enjoy the donuts hot or cold.

Appendix : Recipes Index

Chicken Milanese 28
Chicken Parmesan With Marinara Sauce 22
Chicken Tikka 25
Chilli Lime Tilapia 41
Chocolate Dipped Biscuits 62
Chocolate Orange Muffins 62
Chocolate-glazed Banana Slices 59
Chonut Holes 61
Copycat Fish Fingers 39
Corn Nuts 19
Courgette Fries 5
Crispy Cajun Fish Fingers 42
Crispy Potato Peels 47
Crunchy Chicken Tenders 28
Crunchy Mexican Breakfast Wrap 6
Cumin Shoestring Carrots 9

E

Easy Cheese & Bacon Toasties 7

F

Fillet Mignon Wrapped In Bacon 34
Fish In Foil 43
Fish Taco Cauliflower Rice Bowls 40
French Toast Sticks 60
Fruit Crumble 59

G

Garlic Butter Salmon 40
Garlic Cheese Bread 16
Garlic Tilapia 41
Gluten Free Honey And Garlic Shrimp 37
Grain-free Chicken Katsu 24
Grain-free Millionaire's Shortbread 64
Grilled Bacon And Cheese 53

H

Hamburgers 31
Hasselback New Potatoes 58
Healthy Bang Bang Chicken 21
Healthy Breakfast Bagels 10
Healthy Stuffed Peppers 8

I

Italian Rice Balls 15

Pecan & Molasses Flapjack 63
Pepper & Lemon Chicken Wings 26
Peppers With Aioli Dip 18
Pesto Salmon 39
Pistachio Brownies 62
Pitta Pizza 11
Pizza Chicken Nuggets 20
Plantain Fries 6
Pork Belly With Crackling 30
Pork Chops With Honey 30
Potato & Chorizo Frittata 8
Potato Fries 8
Potato Wedges With Rosemary 57
Pretzel Bites 18

Q

Quick Chicken Nuggets 27

R

Ravioli Air Fryer Style 46
Ricotta Stuffed Aubergine 52
Roast Pork 35
Roasted Almonds 18
Roasted Cauliflower 47
Roasted Okra 55

S

Saganaki 51
Salt & Pepper Calamari 38
Salt And Vinegar Chips 13
Sea Bass With Asparagus Spears 37
Southern Style Pork Chops 35
Spanakopita Bites 48
Special Oreos 61
Spicy Chickpeas 19
Spring Ratatouille 50
Steak Popcorn Bites 29
Sticky Asian Beef 34
Sticky Chicken Tikka Drumsticks 25
Store-cupboard Fishcakes 40
Stuffed Mushrooms 13
Super Easy Fries 54
Sweet & Spicy Baby Peppers 55
Sweet And Sticky Ribs 33
Sweet Potato Tots 52
Sweet Potato Wedges 58

Printed in Great Britain
by Amazon